The
Religious Philosophy
of
William James

The
Religious Philosophy
of
William James

Robert J. Vanden Burgt

Nelson-Hall nh Chicago

To my wife, Connie

Library of Congress Cataloging in Publication Data

Vanden Burgt, Robert J   1936–
   The religious philosophy of William James.

   Bibliography: p.
   Includes index.
   1.   James, William, 1842–1910—Religion.
2.   Religion—Philosophy. I. Title.
B945.J24V36   210   80–22936
ISBN 0–88229–594–2 (cloth)
ISBN 0–88229–767–8 (paper)

Manufactured in the United States of America

10   9   8   7   6   5   4   3   2   1

Contents

Preface

Many books have been written on William James, but little attention has been given to his reflections on religion. This is partly attributable to the fact that he never wrote a work devoted specifically to expressing his own religious views. His writings, however, show a lifelong interest in religious questions—an interest, it should be added, that reflects a deep personal struggle on James' part. The present work draws together the various facets of James' religious thought and presents them in light of what they were for the man himself—an effort to find the fullest possible meaning and value in human life.

I am thankful to many people who have helped me to bring this study to completion. In particular I would like to thank Dean Donald King and St. Norbert College for the sabbatical leave that gave me the opportunity to devote my full attention to the manuscript. I also owe a great debt to Beatrice Zedler of Marquette University, whose generous help over the years has been so important in my study of James. Ken Zahorski, a colleague, has kindly read what I have written and rescued it from a variety of grammatical errors. Peggy Schlapman, as typist and proofreader, has patiently directed her considerable skills to more than one draft of the manuscript. And finally, I would like to thank my wife, Connie. Without her encouragement this project would have been abandoned long before completion.

1.

Introduction

While the name of William James is universally accorded a place of highest prominence in the development of American thought, this prominence is not often associated with his religious philosophy. His greatest and most systematic work, *The Principles of Psychology,* published in 1890, stands as a landmark in the field of psychology. Within the field of philosophy, James is most noted for his contributions to the development of pragmatism. In more recent years, his affinity with phenomenology and existentialism has been documented by a series of books that have focused on particular aspects of *The Principles of Psychology.*[1] None of this, however, at least in any direct way, is concerned with James as a religious thinker.

Yet religion does have an important place in his thought. He once remarked in a letter that religion was the great interest of his life.[2] While this may be an overstatement, there is abundant support in his writings to show that religion is at least one of his primary interests. During the 1880s and 1890s

James wrote a number of essays on matters of faith and morals. These were published in 1897 under the title *The Will to Believe and Other Essays in Popular Philosophy* and later republished, under the editorship of Ralph Barton Perry, as *Essays in Faith and Morals*. *The Varieties of Religious Experience* was published in 1902. This book consisted of James' Gifford lectures of that year and the previous one. As its title suggests, it focuses on religion as experienced in the lives of its adherents, showing essentially the power and vitality it lends to those lives. *Pragmatism* was published five years later, in 1907. The more controversial aspects of this book are not usually associated with religion, but, in fact, one of its major concerns was in offering pragmatism as a philosophy that could lend empirical support to religion.[3] Finally, in 1909, *A Pluralistic Universe* was published. In this book James attempted to work out a theory of reality in support of his own religious conception of the universe. So, overall, questions of religion do have an important place in his writings.

Despite this importance, however, surprisingly little attention has been given to James' religious philosophy. Only one book, published in 1926 and now out of print, has been devoted to this aspect of his thought.[4]

To this lacuna in the literature on James the present volume is addressed. But it would be misleading to say no more than this. For the primary purpose of this book is not to fill a gap in Jamesian scholarship. In fact, it makes no pretension at all to scholarship in the technical sense. Instead, it attempts to offer the insights of James to the many contemporary persons who, in their own lives, are struggling with the same religious questions that plagued him. As we shall see, his reflections on religion are always existential; they are always efforts to deal with these questions in the form in which they actually touch human life. Let me explain these two points further—why his reflections have a particular relevance to the present-day situation, and how they are aimed at helping the flesh-and-blood person deal with his religious problems.

THE CONTEMPORARY CHARACTER OF JAMES' RELIGIOUS PHILOSOPHY

In the last twenty years the questions of the existence of God and of the possibility of meaningful discourse about that God have assumed a central place in theological reflection. The point has been made often enough during this time that the question of the reality of God is the fundamental religious issue, without which there is no other.[5] Now there is nothing strange about philosophers and theologians discoursing on the issue of God's existence. What is new in the present situation is that the problem has emerged within the churches themselves. Previously, the battle was fought by the believers against the forces of agnosticism or atheism, but now very often the believer himself is questioning his own belief. It is not the believer against the unbeliever, but the believer honestly facing up to the element of unbelief within himself. The question in this case is a very personal one, touching deeply the meaning of the lives of those experiencing doubt. It does not admit of solution through abstract philosophical speculation, the actual form that most discussion bearing on the existence of God has taken. Such cerebral discussions seem to have power only over those whose beliefs are already established. Instead, this issue requires reflections more sensitive to the believers' own experiences, reflections which have the power to influence real beliefs precisely because they incorporate into themselves the felt dimension of our lives.

James approaches religious questions in this vein. We find him discussing such topics as man's experience of his own contingent hold upon his life and its meaning, his need for cosmic support in the pursuit of his ideals, and the right of persons to follow their deeply felt tendencies toward religious belief. It is just such reflections which enabled James to come to terms with the religious difficulties in his own life. And it is this sensitivity to the problem as a personal one, one that must be dealt with in humanly satisfying terms, that gives his reflections their interest for us today.

Ralph Barton Perry, whose book *The Thought and Character of William James* is the monument in Jamesian scholarship, affirms the personal character of James' philosophy:

> He had for many years brooded upon the nature of the universe and the destiny of man. Although the problem stimulated his curiosity and fascinated his intellect, it was at the same time a vital problem. He was looking for a solution that should be not merely tenable as judged by scientific standards, but at the same time propitious enough to live by. Philosophy was never, for James, a detached and dispassionate inquiry into truth; still less was it a form of amusement. It was a quest, the outcome of which was hopefully and fearfully apprehended by a soul on trial and awaiting its sentence.[6]

Again, what is of note in this passage is the approach to philosophy as vital enterprise through which man seeks truths by which he may live. In the case of the question of belief in God, to expand a point made in the previous paragraph, this concern took the form of a critical inquiry into those needs in man that press toward the affirmation of God's existence, as well as an appraisal of the religious experiences that seem to testify to it. For James it was the experiential domain, our felt needs and mystical tendencies, that was the source of religious beliefs and their sustaining force. He defended the legitimacy of these experiences to have their say in shaping our beliefs. Also, since the greatest challenge to religious belief came from science, or the scientific mentality, it was necessary to examine the strength of this challenge. Because none of these inquiries can in any definitive intellectual way settle the question of God's existence, it was also necessary to raise the question of what to do in this uncertain circumstance. And here James defended man's right to believe, at least under certain conditions. Together, these different considerations formed a concrete approach to the question of God's existence, and it is this that is characteristic of James' philosophical theism.

With this "philosophy in the service of life" focus to his reflections, James' attention is turned away from issues that have traditionally interested theistic philosophers. The arguments for the existence of God have little interest for him, since they are too abstract and metaphysical to help the individual who is searching for answers which he can personally appropriate. Even were they valid, they would have no persuasive power, but could only fortify the convictions of those whose beliefs spring from other sources. Likewise, a full account of God's attributes, metaphysically elaborated, does not concern James. Of what real interest to the religious person are these attributes if they have no bearing on his relationship to God? Instead, as we saw, James wants to deal with the doubts and aspirations of the living, experiencing person. The real sources of doubt and springs of belief lie embedded more deeply in the human being than in his mere intellect. And so it is with this vital center of the person that James attempts to keep contact.

Lest the above point about the concrete character of James' reflections be taken in an exaggerated form, it should be added that he was as capable as the next philosopher of pursuing his task in a highly speculative fashion, with an interest in truth for its own sake. Perry goes on to add that James, in his more exuberant moments, "relished the play of his speculative and critical faculties, and during long periods of vigorous productivity he became, like any other investigator, interested in special problems for themselves...."[7] And as everyone familiar with philosophy knows, any worthwhile philosopher must establish his position on solid foundations, and the laying of such foundations necessarily involves concerns that, to the layman, seem miles away from any vital issue. So while the central point remains that James was interested in philosophy as a vital enterprise, he also pursued it at times with the abstractness and technicality that characterize so much philosophy. Some of his epistemological and metaphysical essays, such as those collected in *Essays in Radical Empiricism,*[8] are ready evidence of this technical interest.

Neither was the description of James' concrete approach to the problem of God's existence intended as a denunciation of other philosophical means of dealing with this issue. Each philosopher's interests and purposes determine his own way of handling problems as well as his importance for succeeding ages and climates of belief. The contention of the previous remarks was simply that James has a particular relevance to the present situation. Nor should one conclude, as some have, that in making philosophy subservient to life, James has shown himself to be concerned about the value of belief in God rather than in the truth about God's existence. This is too easy a dichotomy. Suffice it to say for now that he was not at all interested in encouraging belief built on anything other than solid grounds. Fuller discussion of this point can profitably be pursued only after looking more thoroughly at James' philosophy. I have raised the issue here only to prevent misinterpretation of what has already been said and to forestall objections that could turn one away from giving James a fair hearing.

I have written at some length about the personal character of James' religious philosophy and of its relationship to the belief situation that many reflective people find themselves in today. But this is not the only respect in which he is linked with present-day concerns. There are other important affinities as well. One of these is the this-worldly character of his religious philosophy. Today, those religious persons touched by our secular culture are asking about the meaning of religion as a formative dimension in their present existence.[9] The question of "the next life" is not completely forgotten, but it has a decidedly secondary place in contemporary discussion. Promises of true happiness and fulfillment in the hereafter do not strike a responsive chord. The more urgent question concerns the meaning of our everyday life. While the Enlightenment ideal of a perfected state of mankind on earth can no longer be seriously entertained, still the focus remains on the achievement of meaning and fulfillment in our present existence. This frame of mind is reflected in contemporary theology in the form of an emphasis upon the immanence of God rather than upon His transcendence. The interest is in exploring how God is present and manifested in the life we are now living. Consequently, the ideal of enduring this temporary travail as a preparation for union with a transcendent God has faded. This same perspective undergirds all of James' thinking. He is concerned with God as an ingredient in our lives now, with how He supports and transforms our existence. Accordingly, his conception of God lays heavy emphasis upon the divine immanence in the world's development. We exist in intimate relationship with this God who no longer rules us from on high.

This leads to what is probably the strongest affinity between James' thinking and much contemporary thinking about God: the matter of human freedom and creativity. Theologians are responding not only to the demands of our secular culture that the meaning of human existence be understood on a "this-worldly" plane, but also to the demand that man be a fully responsible agent in that existence.[10] The traditional attributes of omniscience and omnipotence, which have always posed a problem regarding the freedom of human action, are under scrutiny.[11] More radically, the whole conception of God as a self-existing being, as an "outsider" to human history, is being questioned.[12] One of the impelling forces behind this tendency is precisely the question of what becomes of man and his efforts in a theological scheme wherein God is given the regal dominion that He has enjoyed in traditional theism. Does this conception of God sufficiently allow for man being a truly creative force in shaping the world he lives in? Again, James was sensitive to this issue. One of the hallmarks of his philosophy as a whole is its insistence on giving maximum efficacy to man's endeavors. This is carried over into his theism so that God is conceived in such a way as to respect man's responsibilities in the creation of our world.

None of this is meant to suggest that James has all the answers that present-day theologians are searching for. This would be far from the truth, especially as concerns the delineation of an adequate conception of God. But it does mean that, in his own lifetime and in his own situation, he was facing up to problems that have recently become more widely experienced in the Christian community. Particularly in regard to the question of belief itself we might learn from him. This issue received his greatest attention and consequently is more thoroughly worked out than are the rest of his reflections on religious questions.

THE PLAN OF THIS BOOK

In keeping with the logic of James' own thought, my first concern will be the importance he attributes to belief in God. This will be the matter of the next chapter. James would not be interested in religious questions at all unless belief in God was of importance to human life. He argues that belief is important because it affords support for our living strenuously. This it does by giving our values a significance that they do not have in a materialistic philosophy. He also argues that religious belief is important in providing a meaning to our existence despite the fact that our powers of moral assertion are overcome. And it enables us to "suffer cheerfully" what in other circumstances would be considered tragic or accepted grudgingly.

Given this importance, our concern in chapter three will be with James' effort to make out a case for the reasonableness of belief in God. This is necessary since the value of a belief alone is not sufficient to justify holding it, nor to induce a person to do so. We can't believe nonsense. As we have already seen, this effort to show the reasonableness of belief does not consist in trying to prove the existence of God, although James does argue that the claim of direct, mystical experience of the Divine is one that cannot be discounted. The bulk of his considerations, however, are less direct. He argues against science as the sole determiner of our beliefs by showing that its account of reality arises out of a particular perspective that limits the range of its authority. On the positive side, James maintains that interest and need are at the source of all our beliefs, and that the religious needs have as much right to be heard as any other. And, finally, he argues that, under specific conditions, a person has the right to believe despite the objective uncertainty of his beliefs.

Chapter four takes up the question of the nature of God. James' finite God theory is explained. Of greatest interest are the reasons James offers for maintaining the finitude of the Divine. These show significant similarities to present-day concerns: God must be so conceived as to lend meaning to man's present existence; He must allow man's efforts to have a significant place in determining the nature and outcome of our world; He must have an intimacy with man that is lacking in a more transcendently oriented notion of God, and He must not instate evil in the world as a necessary and inevitable factor.

In chapter five the theme of pragmatism as it affects James' religious philosophy will be dealt with explicitly. Both as a general outlook and as a specific theory of meaning and truth, this pragmatism is manifested in his religious philosophy.

However, one who does not accept the specifics of James' pragmatism can still find much of value in his religious philosophy.

A final chapter will be directed toward an overall evaluation of his efforts as a philosopher of religion. It will also relate his religious concerns to certain developments in theology during this century. James was a forerunner with respect to important theological issues that have surfaced in our time. His contributions lie especially in his helping to bring to conscious awareness tensions that were building between the acceptance of certain traditional religious beliefs and an emerging view of man and the world that posed a challenge to those beliefs.

Finally, a word about the overall character of this book. Since James himself never wrote a unified treatise on his religious philosophy, this work will draw from various sources, ordering them in a manner that is congenial to James' own thinking. Connections will be made that are not explicit in his writings but which are clearly in line with his overall thinking. There will be an effort to dig beneath surface formulas and statements that have invited interpretations which have not done justice to the full depth of his thought. More than most writers, James has left himself open to casual dismissal through his use of phrases and statements that stand out in his writings and offer easy targets for critics. If this work helps to offset such interpretations and begins to show the depth of James' thought, it will have served its purpose. Certainly few readers, if any, will find James' reflections free from points that are disputable. But still his writings display a richness of insight and suggestion that make a consideration of them rewarding.

2.

The Importance of Religious Belief

In *The Varieties of Religious Experience* we find the following striking passage:

> The lustre of the present hour is always borrowed from the background of possibilities it goes with. Let our common experiences be enveloped in an eternal moral order; let our suffering have an immortal significance; let Heaven smile upon the earth, and deities pay their visits; let faith and hope be the atmosphere which man breathes in;—and his days pass by with zest; they stir with prospects, they thrill with remoter values. Place round them on the contrary the curdling cold and gloom and absence of all permanent meaning which for pure naturalism and the popular science evolutionism of our time are all that is visible ultimately, and the thrill stops short, or turns rather to anxious trembling.
>
> For naturalism, fed on recent cosmological speculations, mankind is in a position similar to that of a set of people living on a frozen lake, surrounded by cliffs over which there is no escape, yet knowing that little by little the ice is

melting, and the inevitable day drawing near when the last film of it will disappear, and to be drowned ignominiously will be the human creature's portion. The merrier the skating, the warmer and more sparkling the sun by day, and the ruddier the bonfires by night, the more poignant the sadness with which one must take in the meaning of the total situation.[1]

An exquisite example of James' inimitable philosophic prose and imagination, this passage is more notable for the basic theme it expresses in his religious philosophy. The present life of mankind, when looked at in relation to its ultimate significance, draws its meaning from its relationship to a deeper order of reality. This deeper order gives lasting significance to our present efforts. It supports the value of our causes, and through it we endure the hour of our difficulty. Deprived of an eternal moral order, man's life loses its most basic sustaining force and becomes prey to despair. While this thought is certainly not new with James, he strongly affirmed it and cast it into a shape that suited his own outlook.

Naturalism, growing rapidly in James' day and propelled especially by the overall growth of the natural sciences, entailed the lack of permanent meaning of which James speaks. But it did not do so in the foreboding context described in the passage above. Instead, it carried with it a sense of relief and growth at having overcome ancient dogmas and religious superstitions relating this world to a supernatural order. Man would now be free to create a world in accordance with his own specifications and technological ingenuity. And this release from the supernatural was finally being carried out, not on the basis of airy philosophical speculation, but through an understanding of the implications of solidly established scientific facts and procedures of inquiry.

Why, in the face of this scientific tide of disbelief and emancipation from traditional religious dogmas, did James continue to believe, and to maintain the importance of that belief in the life of man? The answers to these two questions are closely related in his philosophy, and they will eventually be tied together; but for the present let us see why James considers religious belief important to man's life. Contrary to the outlook of many philosophers of the last hundred years, this importance is not restricted to the downtrodden, the not yet matured instances of humanity who still, as the story goes, fail to realize that man must stand on his own two feet. Instead, it is important for anyone who considers the full scope of man's condition in the world. This includes the healthiest of the human species.

RELIGIOUS BELIEF AND THE "STRENUOUS MOOD"

One of the characteristic features of James' outlook on life was his assertion that fundamental to the makeup of man is his need to use his powers toward the attainment of desired goals. And that attainment must be contingent upon man's contributions. Now, in the fulfillment of our everyday needs, this may normally be taken for granted, calling for no extraordinary effort on our part. But man's aspirations can and often do extend beyond the ordinary, to ideal or remote goals. To willingly expend the efforts needed to make possible the realization of these goals is to live strenuously, in what James calls the "strenuous mood." The following passage speaks both of our capacity for this mood and what is needed to arouse it.

> The capacity for the strenuous mood probably lies slumbering in every man, but it has more difficulty in some than in others in waking up. It needs the wilder passions to arouse it, the big fears, loves, and indignations; or else the deeply penetrating appeal of some one of the higher fidelities, like justice, truth, or freedom.[2]

This dedicated sort of living constitutes, in James' view, the fullness of human existence. Perry, in *The Thought and*

Character of William James, characterizes that outlook: "If there is to be anything valuable in living, it must be living of *a certain sort,* in which one both serves a moral ideal and *believes in it.*"[3] Life on this view is a real fight in which we rigorously pursue our basic life values, pursuing them with the conviction that their realization is dependent, at least in part, on us.

The following example, all too realistic, may be used to illustrate James' point. Say it becomes clear that the future of a large segment of the human race is seriously threatened by the world's mushrooming population. Survival demands that economic growth keep pace with the spiraling population. But that growth is challenged on either of two fronts: the world's resources cannot sustain such growth or, if they can, the environmental deterioration accompanying the development necessary for such sustenance threatens to make the earth uninhabitable.[4] Bleakness is the essence of this picture. Only drastic sacrifices and great fortitude can make a satisfactory outcome even possible. How would we respond to this situation?

For some the attitude would be "Whatever will be will be." This is determinism, the belief that events will run their inevitable course with human action simply part of the predetermined scheme. For others, the present should be milked for all it is worth, and the future should be left to take care of itself. For still others, this situation would be the definitive proof that the world is truly a vale of tears, our true destiny being our heavenly home.

Each of these responses would be radically opposed to James' strenuous mood. His response would be one of courage, of fighting for what we want, for the optimum realizable outcome. Life is, or can be, a battle for the realization and maintenance of values of whatever sort; the willingness to fight for these values, with no guarantee of success, is to live in the strenuous mood. It is a calling which demands energy and which may be difficult to sustain over a long period of time. But it is a calling which James felt lay slumbering in each of us, and it is one to which he himself responded in the fitter moments of his life.

There is nothing mysterious here. James is simply calling attention to the fact that we all find in our lives the occasion that calls for the full use of our energies in the pursuit of something we value. For some this may be in the political arena; for others it may be in the area of philosophy, as it was for James. For many more the quiet difficulties that can arise in maintaining cherished values in day-to-day family living may require great energies and powers of persistence. To actively pursue these values, or moral ideals, is to live in the strenuous mood. It is to live life most deeply. The example of human survival used above was an extreme one, but it can be scaled down to a size that fits the deeper values at stake in any life, and then what James means by the strenuous mood is applicable.

We seem to have strayed from our original topic, that of the importance of religious belief, but the detour was a necessary one. For James links the strenuous mood with religious belief. Such belief can provide vital support for the strenuous life. If we see the objects of our energies to be embedded in an eternal moral order they will take on an importance which justifies and sustains our energies. And thus the religious belief in this moral order carries a great importance for human life. Life, at least for many, cannot be lived to its fullest—that is, in the strenuous mood—without such a belief. To better understand this let us look explicitly at some of the essays in which James deals with this issue.

In "The Sentiment of Rationality" James discusses the characteristics, both theoretical and practical, that a philosophy must have to gain wide acceptance. For the present let us ignore the strangeness of this question for the philosopher, whose concern traditionally has been for the truth of a theory and not its appeal. Instead, we shall look at James' considerations in terms of their pertinence to the strenuous mood issue before us. "For a philosophy to succeed on a universal scale," he says, "it must define the future *congruously with our spontaneous powers*."[5] This means that such a philosophy must not disappoint our "dearest desires," but even more importantly, it must provide an adequate outlet for our "most intimate powers." The universe must be conceived of in such a way so as not to leave our aspirations with no chance of fulfillment. It must also make provisions for our own efforts to be determining factors in the outcome of the universe. They must have a "relevancy in universal affairs." In effect, James is spelling out a formula for a universe which justifies man living in the strenuous mood. It gives the fullness of meaning to the objects of his desires and it lays at least part of the responsibility for their realization upon him.

This point can be made more concretely. For one who finds, for example, something worth striving for in peace among nations or an equitable distribution of the world's resources or love among people on a day-to-day basis, there are certain conditions that must be met if the struggle is to be carried on. For one thing, these values must be realizable, at least to a significant extent. They cannot be impossible ideals. And second, our contribution to their realization must be an indispensable one. If we are convinced that what will happen, will happen no matter what our efforts are, then the hour of difficulty will surely find us complacent. Regarding the first point, that of the possibility of these ideals being realized, James maintains that for this to occur they must be supported by the deepest powers in the universe. Continuing with our examples, if one conceives of man as being so intrinsically aggressive or destructive that peace is not possible, or so selfish that an equitable distribution of the world's goods is a pipedream, then we certainly will not find it within our capacities to pursue these goals with any vigor. And even if we allow ourselves the hope that the conditions for the realization of these goals may have fortuitously graced the human race, without a God all these efforts may well come to nought in the long run, or in some larger scheme. God, in other words, is the assurance that the conditions necessary for the realization of our ideals are present, and that if we work at it, these ideals can be realized. God guarantees not that our ideals will be realized, but that such conditions exist that our efforts can be successful if pursued. In short, the universe is a place wherein man's efforts strike a responsive chord, a place wherein ideals are realizable and have a place within a context of ultimate meaning.

Admittedly, such considerations place man's life in a perspective of ultimacy which is not always present in our day-to-day consciousness. We are usually carried along by our more immediate motives, oblivious to deeper reference, and content with daily satisfactions. But James is thinking of life in its more demanding element—as he says, in the strenuous mood. And it is in this context that we are more apt to reflect upon the final worth of our efforts. Here it becomes important whether we see man as a temporary occurrence in a mindless evolutionary scheme, or as central to the meaning of the entire process. Moreover, James is interested in formulating a creed which is adequate to sustain us in the "lonely emergencies of life." How must the world be conceived so as to provide the support we need in our more trying and desperate moments? A creed adequate to our sunny days may be quite inadequate in our darker hours.

This does not necessarily mean that any belief short of God will lead to despair in hard times. James saw the value of stoical resignation and of man asserting himself simply through defying his fate, however much suffering it may involve. There is dignity in this. Thus, life is not without value in a world without God. But God adds so much. Our values resonate with those of the universe as a whole. Our efforts have cosmic significance. With God, life can be lived on a new level, with fullest significance and purpose. A philosophy which falls short of supporting this belief is one which entails a much diminished view of our place in the universe.

Thus, a theistic philosophy best supports the strenuous mood. It gives man's values a stable place in the universe. And contrary to deterministic absolutism, it can be so conceived as to make their furtherance dependent upon man. Materialism falls short. "For materialism denies reality to the objects of almost all the impulses we most cherish."[6] The result: "A nameless 'unheimlichkeit' comes over us at the thought of there being nothing eternal in our final purposes, in the objects of those loves and aspirations which are our deepest energies."[7] Such a universe does not provide the sustaining basis for man to live strenuously because the value of the achievable results is subject to question. Man's interests are cosmic trivia, insignificant in the ultimate scheme of things, and finally reducible to the mere interplay of materialistic forces. How do we generate the energy to work toward long-range and demanding goals if nothing lasting is achieved in the process?

Obviously, James' position raises a good many sceptical questions. Does man have a deep-seated need to live in the strenuous mood? Is a belief in an eternal moral order really necessary for sustaining the strenuous life? Is this true for all men, or only some? And even if religion is important in the life of mankind does that justify belief in its basic tenets? These issues will be taken up shortly, but for the present let us consider one further essay in which James discusses the strenuous mood.

"The Moral Philosopher and the Moral Life" is the only treatise James ever wrote devoted exclusively to ethical issues. In it he inquires into the meaning of the words *obligation* and *good,* and he also attempts to settle the question of the order of human obligations. In the course of this essay he affirms the point that a system of ethical obligation is certainly possible without a God, but in the final section he considers the relationship between ethical obligation, belief in God, and the strenuous mood.

In contrast to the previous essay we considered, James here emphasizes less the fulfillment possible in a theistic universe and more the demands placed on us in such a universe. Not only does a theistic conception of the universe provide an adequate basis for justifying the strenuous mood, but the universe, theistically conceived, can also be seen as demanding and eliciting that mood from us. Why so? Without an "infinite demander" our values are no more than matters of human preference. This is important, to be sure, but not enough. To return to the survival of mankind example considered earlier, we might ask whether concern for future generations will be enough to generate the required sacrifices on everyone's part? Will we face present difficulties and tragedies in such a way as to secure and perpetuate the values we consider important in our lives? James says a "don't care" or easygoing attitude would be easy to adopt in such cases were the only demands those of possible future generations. Referring to a religion of humanity he says:

> Many of us . . . would openly laugh at the very idea of the strenuous mood being awakened in us by these claims of remote posterity which constitute the last appeal of the religion of humanity. . . . This is all too finite, we say; we see too well the vacuum beyond. It lacks the note of infinitude and mystery, and may all be dealt with in the don't-care mood. . . .
>
> When however we believe that a God is there, and that he is one of the claimants, the infinite perspective opens up. The scale of the symphony is incalculably prolonged.[8]

In a theistic universe obligations occur touching not just transitory and negligible matters, but relating instead to the deepest and most final purposes conceivable. To view our place in the world in this light opens us up to inexhaustible sources of energy and courage.

Our attitude towards concrete evils is entirely different in
a world where we believe there are none but finite de-
manders, from what it is in one where we joyously face
tragedy for an infinite demander's sake. Every sort of energy and endurance, of courage and capacity for handling
life's evils, is set free in those who have religious faith.[9]

The strenuous mood then requires a belief in God. In his
deepest self man wants to live strenuously, but this can be sufficiently justified only in a universe where our needs will not
be frustrated and our energies wasted. In a theistic universe
this is the case as man's need to live strenuously coincides
with the demand from the infinite that he do so. So belief in
such a universe is of vital importance for man's life.

What is peculiar about the position of James sketched
above is the hardiness it attributes to the believer. God is an
energizing force in life, supporting our own strenuous efforts.
This is not the role He is ordinarily thought to play in the
believer's life. More often one thinks of religion in terms of the
comfort and security the believer receives. Thus, for example,
when my best efforts seem to get me nowhere, when I fail
miserably and am fit for despair, I may find solace in knowing
that in the eyes of Him who really matters I am not guilty. In
another vein the God of providence may be one who assures
me that whatever hardships I may endure, these are elements
within a wider scheme wherein justice and righteousness are
destined to prevail. Thus, God rescues man from guilt or fate
as the case may be. He saves us despite our own powerlessness.

One might think that James, given his strenuous life notion,
would have little patience with such a religious outlook. After
all, while it may conceive of the universe religiously, it does
so in a way that is incompatible with his own understanding
of what human life at its best is all about. But James does not
reject the passive fruits of religion, at least not without recognizing their value for a certain class of religious persons. He

is sympathetic to their importance since man is not simply a creature of the strenuous constitution, but a creature of weakness as well. Life, conceived of as a struggle, can overwhelm us and leave us with the simple need that all shall be taken care of by some higher power. And this need may be as insistent as that of living in the strenuous mood. James' views on this point will round out our consideration of the importance he attributes to religious belief.

Religious Belief as a Saving Faith

It was in *The Varieties of Religious Experience* that James dealt most fully with the importance of a saving faith. The man of faith here is not thought of as needing God to sustain his moral earnestness or vigor. Rather, God rescues him amidst his own impotencies or, more positively, He is an active, living presence to him. This takes many forms. The sick soul must be rescued from sheer meaninglessness, or from guilt and damnation. God's saving grace converts the wayward from perverse lives to righteousness. The saint lives his life in the conscious presence of God, surrenders himself to that higher controlling power, and makes spiritual progress toward the breakdown of the confines of selfhood. The mystic experiences the grace of God as he is lifted to an ineffable union with Him. He knows God with a directness and overwhelmingness that radically surpasses all modes of ordinary knowing. Such is the God who saves and who falls within the varieties of religious experience.

God, as so experienced, can also be a transformer of attitudes in a way that isn't possible when He is conceived of solely as an ally of the moral ideals to which we are committed. A person ultimately secure in the hands of God can accept the world and his place in it, including suffering, with an enthusiastic assent that surpasses the burdensome feeling sometimes experienced in attempting to secure a righteous moral order. We can, if necessary, face suffering joyfully as embodying the will of God for us. God is all and we are nothing.

> There is a state of mind, known to religious men, but to no others, in which the will to assert ourselves and hold our own has been displaced by a willingness to close our mouths and be as nothing in the floods and waterspouts of God. In this state of mind, what we most dreaded has become the habitation of our safety, and the hour of our mortal death has turned into our spiritual birthday. The time for tension in our soul is over, and that of happy relaxation, of calm deep breathing, of an eternal present, with no discordant future to be anxious about, has arrived. Fear is not held in abeyance as it is by mere morality, it is positively expunged and washed away.[10]

James goes on to add that when religion enables one to suffer and sacrifice gladly it *"makes easy and felicitous what is in any case necessary*: and if it be the only agency that can accomplish this result, its vital importance as a human faculty stands vindicated beyond dispute."[11]

Such a state obviously represents the fullness of depth and expression that religion can reach in the lives of its adherents. Not everyone reaches the point of "dancing in the flames," but more modest levels of conviction and attitude are still of vital importance to many lives. To experience decisive frustration in our efforts, or prolonged sufferings in our lives, or powerful and final wrenches in our human relationships can leave the best of men prey to brooding melancholy. Those for whom religion can offer some saving grace from this distraught state, even if it falls far short of joyful acceptance, are also persons for whom religion is vitally important.

In *Pragmatism,* James joins the saving faith of *The Varieties* with the theory of absolutism in philosophy, again recognizing its value for human life. Absolutism, involving determinism as it does, is of value insofar as it affords man an occasional moral holiday, a respite from the strenuous mood. James speaks sympathetically of this need.

> There are moments of discouragement in us all, when we are sick of self and tired of vainly striving. Our own life breaks down, and we fall into the attitude of the prodigal son. We mistrust the chances of things. We want a universe where we can just give up, fall on our father's neck, and be absorbed into the absolute life as a drop of water melts into the river or sea.[12]

Religion in this state of paralysis of moral energy provides a refuge from the demands of life. Our life is not bankrupt despite our inability to further our causes.

Religion, then, has a twofold importance—one wherein it supplies a needed support for the moral will, and the other an importance based on God as a saving power in life. The first is a support for man in an active mood, the second in a passive mood. James was sensitive to the needs of man in each of these cases and so extolled the merits of religion on each count. This did not, however, blind him to the fact that the religious universes required to satisfy these two needs were largely incompatible, and that the individual thinker, in the interests of consistency, had to choose between them. The universe of the strenuous mood was a morally demanding one, not yet determined in its outcome, but depending upon the contributions of its individual members to achieve this or that result. The universe of the sick soul, on the other hand, especially in its more extreme form of seeking total refuge in the absolute, was fully predetermined. The cares of the religious soul are taken account of and secured without the effort of will demanded in the strenuous mood.

James himself was both a sick soul and morally invigorated at different points in his life. But all commentators on his philosophy agree that his more characteristic gospel was that of the strenuous mood. An overall reading of his writings strongly conveys this impression, though from beginning to end one is struck by his sensitivity to the ambiguity of the human situation and its potential for tragedy. Still, James was a man of moral vigor and his deeper self was realized in this more assertive form. In a letter of self-analysis, written in the middle years of his life, he states that a man's true character is shown when, in a particular mental or moral attitude, he feels himself most intensely alive. He goes on to point out that in his own case "this characteristic attitude . . . always involves an element of active tension, of holding my own, as it were, and trusting outward things to perform their part so as to make it a full harmony; but without a *guaranty* that they will."[13] Were there to be such a guaranty, James adds, reality would lose its sting and man's importance as a contributor to the moral life of the universe would diminish proportionately. In his healthier moods James was unwilling to accept any such diminished stature for man.

THE SUPPORT FOR JAMES' POSITION

It is now time to return to the questions we raised earlier, which are still unanswered, and which, if anything, have grown even more pressing. Might it not be that persons seeking the support of religion in either of the capacities discussed are enfeebled human creatures who have not yet come alive to the contemporary vision of autonomous man? Isn't religion essentially a form of human weakness, carried over into the present scientifically understood and technologically dominated world from the prior world of ignorance, superstition and helplessness? In short, isn't religion for the present-day liberated person of no real importance, and are not its adherents really suffering from a hangover growing out of the human situation of a previous age? And more importantly, even if religion could be shown to have importance for men today, this by no means, of itself, justifies religious belief. Religion still may be nothing but opium, even if the dosage is still needed by many. But in that case, does not human integrity demand a clear view of man's place in the universe, and a commitment to living it lucidly? Believing because we want a God is mere wishful thinking, unworthy of a mature outlook.

Two basic questions are involved here. The first concerns the alleged importance of religion, and the second the justification for belief in God. We will discuss the first of these questions in the remainder of this chapter and the second question in the next.

First, concerning the question of the importance of belief, a number of considerations are in order. It is apparent from daily observation that, factually speaking, not everyone needs religion as a sustaining force in his life. Religion here means an explicit belief that reality in its ultimate form is disposed toward the fostering of man's deepest interests. Many men do live strenuously without that support. Others undergo great sufferings and failure and yet live on meaningfully without God. James' colleague in promoting philosophical pragmatism, John Dewey, is an outstanding example of someone who led such a strenuous life. He was untiringly dedicated to fostering a social world wherein the quality of human life would be enhanced. This struggle he carried on without reliance on the deeper support which the religious person seeks. So it is simply a matter of psychological fact that the vital importance of religion that James speaks of does not touch every life. Certainly James, as an observer of the human scene, knew this.

Yet, there are all those persons, who, for whatever reasons of background or religious sensitivity, find a purely naturalistic scheme of things too superficial a view of life's meaning. Again, speaking factually, for these persons religion is important. Which of these two views, the one finding the ordinary motivation and supports of life adequate, or the other demanding an eternal dimension to our efforts, is the more satisfactory response to the human situation? Does either of these two views overlook important elements in the human situation taken into account by the other? This is more than a question of how people do in fact feel. It raises the evaluative question as to the merits of these contrasting outlooks in terms of their adequacy in understanding the human condition in which man finds himself.

As in all philosophical questions there is no likelihood of finding any universally agreed upon answer to this question. The push and pull of life is experienced differently by people given such factors as their varied backgrounds, their different experiences in their mature years, and their more active or more reflective natures. This produces different perspectives on life. Nonetheless, within reasonable boundaries we should be able to judge whether any particular view is at least making a respectable claim. With this caution in mind let us return to James' own view.

As one would expect, he himself certainly considered the religious perspective to be the more profound one. What led him to this conviction? Although, as we said, the full answer to this question is hidden in the deeper resources of any given individual, we know enough about James' life to suggest a partial answer. His own father was a troubled religious soul, and a mystic of sorts, who eventually found his salvation in the religion of Swedenborg. Not surprisingly, he created a home atmosphere wherein the question of man's place in the universe was accorded central importance. While the son did not share his father's undiluted passion for religious questions, he was an individual who, in his own experience, had touched bottom in life. When he was twenty-eight years old he suffered an extended period of severe depression. The anhedonia he describes in *The Varieties of Religious Experience* was his own lot as well as that of others.

He was afflicted by a complete "loss of appetite for life's values." And he seriously considered suicide as the resolution for his ills. This period of depression reached its extremity in an experience of "panic fear" which James described in *The Varieties*. Though he attributed it in that book to a French correspondent, he later confessed it to be his own:

> Whilst in this state of philosophic pessimism and general depression of spirits about my prospects, I went one evening into a dressing-room in the twilight to procure some article that was there; when suddenly there fell upon me without any warning, just as if it came out of the darkness, a horrible fear of my own existence. Simultaneously there arose in my mind the image of an epileptic patient whom I had seen in the asylum, a black-haired youth with greenish skin, entirely idiotic, who used to sit all day on one of the benches, or rather shelves against the wall, with his knees drawn up against his chin, and the coarse gray undershirt, which was his only garment, drawn over them inclosing his entire figure. He sat there like a sort of sculptured Egyptian cat or Peruvian mummy, moving nothing but his black eyes and looking absolutely non-human. This image and my fear entered into a species of combination with each other. *That shape am I,* I felt, potentially. Nothing that I possess can defend me against that fate, if the hour for it should strike for me as it struck for him. There was such a horror of him, and such a perception of my merely momentary discrepancy from him, that it was as if something hitherto solid within my breast gave way entirely, and I became a mass of quivering fear. After this the universe was changed for me altogether. I awoke morning after morning with a horrible dread at the pit of my stomach, and with a sense of the insecurity of life that I never knew before, and that I have never felt since. It was like a revelation; and although the immediate feelings passed away, the experience has made me sympathetic with the morbid feelings of others ever since. It gradually faded, but for months I was unable to go out into the dark alone.[14]

James goes on to add "that if I had not clung to scripture-texts like 'The eternal God is my refuge,' etc., 'Come unto me, all ye that labor and are heavy-laden,' etc., 'I am the resurrection and the life,' etc., I think I should have gone really insane."[15] In this experience James came to realize in an intense and penetrating way the fragile character of human existence. We are separated from nothingness by only the thinnest of margins. And ultimately we are powerless to protect ourselves from such a destiny should it call.

For one subject to such an experience, it is hardly surprising that a sense of the ultimate nothingness of all things having no deeper anchor than the human should continue to be an abiding part of his vision of things. In *The Varieties,* written thirty years after the occurrence of the experience described above, we find James saying:

> The sanest and the best of us are of one clay with lunatics and prison inmates, and death finally runs the robustest of us down. And whenever we feel this, such a sense of the vanity and provisionality of our voluntary career comes over us that all our morality appears but as a plaster hiding a sore it can never cure, and all our well-doing as the hollowest substitute for that well-*being* that our lives ought to be grounded in, but alas! are not.[16]

This is a bland statement compared to his description of "panic fear," but it conveys much the same perspective as that earlier experience. Similar statements can be found in other parts of James' writings, showing his continued sense of the insufficiency of human life left to its own resources.

While this outlook might seem to be the basic ingredient necessary to the creation of the sick-souled religious person, a little reflection shows that it could also cast a religious dimension over a life lived in the strenuous mood. For such an outlook need not drain away all one's energies; it only underlines the fact that the human estate of itself is not enough. And, thus, however one lives his life, he will continue to see it as depending for sufficient worth on a deeper order than the human. Our energies will be in proportion to the ultimate stability of our values.

It seems impossible to deny the validity of this insight—that without God, man's life loses its oneness with the basic nature of things and becomes subject to ultimate tragedy and nothingness. It is the same insight that religious souls down through the ages have experienced. This is not to say that everyone will be equally sensitive to it. To be sure, its power over different persons, or over the same person at different moments in his life, varies. And to others, it may seem to mean nothing. Many are occupied with the immediate satisfactions afforded in day-to-day living, and in that state they are immune from more ultimate considerations. Others, firmly convinced of the truth of atheism, pay no heed to any religious needs, since these needs have no chance of being met anyway. For them it is folly to think of such matters, just as it is folly to wish for a Santa when one's Christmas budget is depleted. For still others, unconditional importance is attached to some particular goal, such as the progress of man or the accumulation of goods, and this satisfies them, at least for a time. However, the fact that the religious perspective is foreign to the outlook of some does not make it any less vital to others. It only says that various circumstances of life may render some persons immune or nonreceptive to the needs which others experience deeply. Yet, these are true needs for those who remain open to them and whose experiences sensitize them to this dimension of life.

To return more specifically to our discussion of James, it would be misleading if one took the above portrayal of James as indicating that his life was one of unrelieved melancholy or brooding over the human condition. Such is far from the truth. True, it was in the "lonely emergencies of life" that his creed was shaped and tested, but that does not mean that his life was nothing but lonely emergencies. He lived a satisfying life, filled with exuberances as well as suffering. He was dedicated to the securing of truth in the philosophical arena, and he fought zealously to give the doctrine of pragmatism a fair hearing. In short, his life was a fulfilling one. The essential point to be gained from looking at James' own background and experiences is that, through them, he was sharply challenged regarding the meaning of human life. And he found it lacking when considered simply in human terms. Thus, his creed was ultimately a religious one. Were this lack not brought home to him through his personal situation in life, he might have remained oblivious to it, energized to whatever degree by the buoyant forces of our natural life. And such surely is the case for countless citizens of the world. But for one sensitized to life's insufficiencies by the circumstances of his life, that option is no longer available and religious belief becomes important. Without it the meaning of our existence would be radically diminished.

Our considerations have taken on a somewhat biographical character in attempting to evaluate the adequacy of James' appraisal of the human condition. To some this might seem like an avoidance of the issue since the question appears to be one of truth or falsity, rather than one of biography. But that is too simply a dichotomy. Meaningful possibilities or depths of human existence may be opened up to us by the testimony of another man's life, lived intensely and reflectively. It is through our own experience, or through the experience of one for whom we feel a spiritual kinship, that our creeds are shaped. This is not to say they are shaped independently of thought, but the intellect is far from their only determinant. Experience is wider than thought and a more telling teacher. James himself maintained that a person's philosophy is to a large extent autobiographical, and so it is appropriate that his own insights should be related to the experiences of his life.

A more specific criticism can be made of James' position. We have seen that the perspective present in his experience of panic fear remained with him throughout his life. If that experience was a formative element in his religious outlook do we not have grounds for dismissing that religion? Such an experience is one that few of the world's citizens are subject to, and it no doubt was brought on by the morbid state of mind which had afflicted James for some time prior to the experience. Isn't it reasonable then to dismiss it as a product of a temporarily deranged mind rather than to make it a cornerstone of one's religious philosophy? To this James himself replied an emphatic no. He devoted the whole of his first chapter in *The Varieties of Religious Experience* to refuting such a contention. There he maintained that the reliability of an experience cannot be judged on the basis of the factors that go into its genesis. Instead, we must look to such considerations as its "immediate luminousness" and "philosophical reasonableness." Who is to say that the deeper insights into the meaning of life must originate in the confines of ordinary consciousness? Certainly they cannot contradict data from that sphere, but extraordinary states of consciousness might open the mind to levels of reality not otherwise knowable. If there is a supernatural dimension of reality it would not be surprising if our consciousness were open to it only in extraordinary moments.

All this goes far beyond the point at hand since James himself never had any experiences of the supernatural. Nonetheless, it is pertinent to the extent that it argues that an experience cannot be dismissed as cognitively insignificant simply because it is of an extraordinary sort. Thus James' own experience could legitimately be given considerable significance for him. This whole point will be more fully explored in the next chapter of James' defense of religious belief.

The overall conclusion that emerges from this chapter is that religious belief is of fundamental importance to human life when that life is viewed in its ultimate setting. This importance is not due to any inability to overcome a distorted perspective. Instead, it is based on a profound and defensible view of human life that seeks deeper support for human values than naturalism allows. Its insight into the human condition is the most telling one.

> Religious melancholy is not disposed of by a simple flourish of the word insanity. The absolute things, the last things, the overlapping things, are the truly philosophic concerns; all superior minds feel seriously about them, and the mind with the shortest views is simply the mind of the more shallow man.[17]

Religious belief, then, is of bona fide importance.

Before moving on, let us take a summary look at where we have been. James finds religious belief of importance for persons of two different constitutions. The person of robust moral energy needs a God to confer depth on his own purposes by aligning them with an eternal moral order. The world, objectively considered, must be responsive to the demands he places upon it, and it must be so in its final makeup. God is the name we give to such an objectively moral order. The sick soul, on the other hand, requires assurance that his needs are already cared for by a deeper power in the universe. God here is not an ally in the causes for which he works; instead He is the one who guarantees his well-being, no matter what trials or failures life brings. James himself, although suffering from his helpless moments, was more the person of moral energy, and he conceived of God accordingly. I suggested that the religious perspective, or perspective of ultimacy, in which James saw life was partially accounted for by his personal experience of the contingency of human existence. And I argued that the consequent importance of religious belief expressed by the religious person was a valid one, since it was based on a defensible view of the human condition.

The importance that James gives to religion is an importance that it can have not only for the underprivileged citizens of life, but also for its best and most sensitive creatures. Here he departs radically from those who would say that religion is important only for that class of persons who have not yet reached full human maturity. Quite the contrary may be true. This still leaves open the question, however, of the rationality of religious belief. The simple fact that we might like something to be true is of itself no good reason to believe that it is. Our needs might not be met in this universe. Let us turn, then, to the question of how James supports the credibility of religious belief.

3.

Grounds for Belief in God

To adequately understand James' defense of religious belief a number of points must be considered. First among them is his rejection of science as an adequate judge of the full range of human beliefs. This rejection is best understood in the context of James' teleological theory of the mind, a theory which portrays the mind as an active and selective agency. That theory in turn helps us to understand his defense of need as a source of belief in God. James further offers an analysis of religious experience and a theory of the "will to believe" as support for this belief. Finally, his rejection of proofs for God's existence enables us to see why that route to the Deity was unavailable to him.

THE RELATION OF RELIGION AND SCIENCE

For James any acceptable defense of religious belief had to come to terms with the naturalism of his day, which was an outgrowth of the scientific spirit and the beneficiary of science's prestige. Science could not be ignored, whether that meant heeding those discoveries that conflicted with religion, or determining the rightful extent of its authority over our beliefs. James was particularly sensitive to this challenge since he himself was thoroughly grounded in the natural sciences. In 1861, he had entered the Lawrence Scientific School at Harvard where he studied chemistry and biology, and eventually received a degree in medicine. His teachers there were some of the scientific luminaries of the day, the most noted being Louis Agassiz. James was one of the students who accompanied Agassiz on his much publicized Brazilian expedition to collect biological species for the Harvard laboratory. Though James soon turned away from the formal study of chemistry and biology, and never did practice medicine, he did remain a student of science. This is easily evidenced in his greatest work, *The Principles of Psychology,* published in 1890, which shows a full awareness of the latest scientific studies of man. In short, James was acquainted with science not simply as a general observer but on an intimate basis. Thus, any religious beliefs that he accepted would have to pass through the rigors of scientific scrutiny. His writings show a continued sensitivity to this challenge.

What was the real nature of the challenge that science posed for religious belief? First of all, its findings challenged certain traditional religious dogmas and grounds for belief. Darwin's *Origin of Species,* for example, created difficulties for accepting man as a direct and special creation of God; the theory of evolution also undermined the argument for God's existence based on design in nature. The challenge to particular dogmas was of no great concern to James since his own religious thinking, based on philosophical considerations as it was, paid little heed to the "revealed truths" of Christianity. And the demise of proofs of God's existence simply meant the abandoning of considerations which already had become ineffectual in producing and maintaining belief. A deeper challenge, and one which did concern James, came in another form. This was the naturalism, or positivism, spawned by an infatuation with science, giving it full jurisdiction over our beliefs. Here the contention was that science offered *the* objective account of reality, while religion was simply a matter of subjective preference, with no real claim to truth. The acceptability of any belief was to be judged by scientific standards. Only what could be expressed and made intelligible in scientific terms could be accepted by a person of intellectual integrity. Here science, or more accurately, some interpreters of science, attempted to extend its domain to the full range of acceptable truths. Science not only expressed its own understanding of the world, but ruled out any effort to go beyond what it said. Thus, if God, or free will, had no place in the scientific scheme, that is, were not discussible within the range of intelligibility allowed by the presuppositions governing the scientific account of reality, belief in them could not be held by an intelligent and informed person. It was this pretension which James attacked vigorously, but only after a struggle in which he was its uncomfortable captive.[1]

Before looking at his response to this challenge it is worth noting that James' thinking was affected by another less direct dimension of the challenge of science to religion. His entire religious philosophy accommodates itself to this challenge, and this accommodation constitutes one of its pervasive characteristics. In his opening chapter in *Pragmatism,* entitled "The Present Dilemma in Philosophy," James says: "Never were as many men of a decidedly empiricist proclivity in existence as there are in the present day. Our children, one may say, are almost born scientific."[2] James would certainly include himself among those of whom he spoke. Given this estimate of the intellectual orientation of his day, any philosophy, to have an impact, must be of an empirical sort. Justification of religious belief based on abstract metaphysical considerations could gain no widespread support, and ran counter to James' own empiricist proclivity. The result was that his religious philosophy counted for its support on the data of experience, but experience understood in a broader sense than science allowed. There were specifically religious experiences and those of moral need that had to be counted in a total view of reality. And James did this. Thus, he espoused no narrow scientism, but the influence of science that did continue to exert itself over his philosophy was in the creation of an intellectual atmosphere wherein the only basis on which to erect a philosophical position was an empirical one.

Accepting this, however, did not mean accepting naturalism. How then did James counter the challenge of science in its pretension to being the sole arbiter of truth about reality? Early in his intellectual life he was inclined to accept the sufficiency of the scientific account of the world. We know from his correspondence that he could not easily see his way out of atheism, uncongenial as it was to his total nature. And regarding his understanding of man he wrote in 1869 that he felt that "we are Nature through and through, that we are wholly conditioned, that not a wiggle of our will happens save as a result of physical laws. . . ."[3] The spell of this scientific view of man was broken a year later through James' reading of the French voluntarist philosopher, Renouvier, who was destined to be one of the abiding influences in James' philosophical development.

What enabled James to break loose from the dominion of science? Essentially, he came to see that the enterprise of science was no disinterested, purely objective account of the nature of the world. Instead, it was based on a desire to give an explanation of things in terms that satisfied particular subjective interests and needs that we have. If this was true, why must the interests which it satisfied be given a priority over other interests, those of a moral nature, which we also want satisfied? Put in this framework, its privileged status as offering an exhaustive account of the world need no longer be accepted.

This is a bold position. To speak of science as anything but a fully objective account of the world, an account which tells us what is "really there," seems like an exercise in wishful thinking taken up by a closed-minded apologist for a religious cause. After all, science has developed a method for the discernment of truth, a method which does away with the capriciousness of individual opinion by ultimately testing any hypothesis through commonly accepted processes of verification. And the truths that have emerged through this process of inquiry have further enhanced their stature by providing the basis for a technological control of our world which has literally transformed present-day life. Given this situation, the prestige of science is entirely understandable, and any effort to demean its office as bearer of the truth about reality deserves suspicion. It is important, then, to look more closely at James' critical analysis.

In his philosophical essays written in the 1880s and 1890s James returns often to the theme that science as a whole is a product of desire, of man carrying through on a particular subjective interest that he has.

> Without an imperious inner demand on our part for ideal logical and mathematical harmonies, we should never have attained to proving that such harmonies lie hidden between all the chinks and interstices of the crude natural world. Hardly a law has been established in science, hardly a fact ascertained, which was not first sought after, often with sweat and blood, to gratify an inner need.[4]

Our interest is in conceiving the world as showing certain connections not manifest in the given sensible world. It is an inner demand on our part which insists that such connections must be there, and it is this faith which sustains us in our inquiry. The resulting scientific account of the world terminates in a conception of nature which is anything but a duplication of the given order. This is so because our own subjective nature demands that we conceive of reality in a form imposed on it by ourselves.

> As if "science" itself were anything else than such an end of desire, and a most peculiar one at that! And as if the "truths" of bare physics in particular, which these sticklers for intellectual purity contend to be the only uncontaminated form, were not as great an alteration and falsification of the simple "given" order of the world, into an order conceived solely for the mind's convenience and delight, as any theistic doctrine possibly can be![5]

And finally:

> I myself believe that all the magnificent achievements of mathematical and physical science—our doctrines of evolution, of uniformity of law, and the rest—proceed from our indomitable desire to cast the world into a more rational shape in our minds than the shape into which it is thrown there by the crude order of our experience. The world has shown itself, to a great extent, plastic to this demand of ours for rationality.[6]

James is making the same point in each of these three passages taken from different essays. The scientific mind is no blank recorder of fact. It manifests a desire on our part to understand the world in a certain fashion. Science approaches reality in an effort to give an account of it showing particular logical and mathematical harmonies. It makes demands on nature; it seeks a particular type of rationality, a particular order and connection in the events of nature. The success of science has been in proportion to the extent that nature has shown itself receptive to such demands.

It is important not to misconstrue the point James is making here. He is not calling into question the impartiality of the method employed by science in verifying or falsifying hypotheses. He accepts that method as the glory of science and incorporates it into his own philosophy. But while its method in settling issues within its domain is a model of impartiality, that does not mean that science as a whole, the scientific enterprise as such, is more than a partial account of reality. It is partial, not full and exhaustive, because it issues from particular interests we have. If we have other interests as well, they have as much right to be given a hearing as do scientific ones. The privileged status that some would like to accord to science stems from the fruitfulness of its method in answering the questions it asks. But this should not be mistaken to mean that it asks all the questions there are to be asked, nor that man must restrict himself in his beliefs to answers it can provide.

The significance of this point for James' religious philosophy lies in the fact that, if the scientific project is an effort to satisfy demands that the human subject places on the world, there is no reason why demands must be limited to this sort. Put somewhat differently, why must the account of the world that satisfies my scientific demands be taken as an exhaustive account of the world when, in fact, I have demands that are not at all satisfied by the scientific account? Why must this account be taken as privileged, as exhaustive? If I am free to try to satisfy my demand for a world that is scientifically intelligible, why am I not free to try to satisfy my demand for a morally or religiously intelligible world as well? James insists on this right. These demands may find nature as receptive as it has been to the demands for scientific intelligibility.[7]

> And if needs of ours outrun the visible universe, why *may* not that be a sign that an invisible universe is there? What, in short, has authority to debar us from trusting our religious demands? Science as such assuredly has no authority, for she can only say what is, not what is not; and the agnostic "thou shalt not believe without coercive sensible evidence" is simply an expression (free to anyone to make) of private personal appetite for evidence of a certain peculiar kind.[8]

And again:

> If a certain formula for expressing the nature of the world
> violates my moral demand, I shall feel as free to throw it
> overboard, or at least doubt it, as if it disappointed my de-
> mand for uniformity of sequence, for example; the one de-
> mand being, so far as I can see, quite as subjective and
> emotional as the other is.[9]

James goes on to add that not only does science have no exclusive right to assert demands, but were we to proceed as if
it did, it would be positively harmful.

> But if the religion of exclusive scientificism should ever
> succeed in suffocating all other appetites out of a nation's
> mind, and imbuing a whole race with the persuasion that
> simplicity and consistency demand a "tabula rasa" to be
> made of every notion that does not form part of the "soi-
> disant" scientific synthesis, that nation, that race, will just
> as surely go to ruin, and fall prey to their more richly con-
> stituted neighbors, as the beasts of the field, as a whole,
> have fallen prey to man.[10]

In short, life would be too much narrowed.

None of this should be taken to mean that religious claims
to truth can ignore the truths established in science. Certainly
a man should not live in contradiction, holding to religious
beliefs which clash with what he holds to be scientifically true.
But this does not preclude the possibility of accepting beliefs
rooted in different kinds of demands that we make on the
world. James asks only that one demand, the scientific one,
not be treated as the only one.

He thus worked himself clear from the claims of positivism,
and remained satisfied with this solution for the rest of his life.
This is not surprising, since the basis for his rejection of positivism is deeply rooted in his overall thinking. It lies in his
conception of the mind as active and interested, rather than
as a *tabula rasa,* a passive recorder of fact. The mind is a

selective agency. It goes toward the world with its own interests and carves the world accordingly. What we have seen above, his rejection of positivism, is simply one manifestation of this more fundamental view of the nature of mind.

This view of the mind not only provides the basis for James' rejection of an exclusive scientism, but it also serves as the fundamental support of his positive advocacy of religious belief. It is a notion that is fundamental to his whole philosophy. Perry, in fact, calls it, "the idea of the essentially active and interested character of the human mind," the "one germinal idea from which his whole thought grew. . . ."[11] Since this idea is so crucial to James' philosophical position, and especially since it stands out in the development of his religious philosophy, it is important to explore it more fully before moving into the positive grounds for religious belief.

THE TELEOLOGICAL MIND

In *The Principles of Psychology* James states early that "the study of the phenomena of consciousness which we shall make throughout the rest of this book will show us that consciousness is at all times primarily a *selecting agency*."[12] This is true at all levels, from the senses to abstract intellection, so that in our entire mental life it is selection based upon interest which sets the limits as to what shall be part of our conscious life. The mind is no passive receptor, but instead approaches the world with particular interests, and these interests determine what will enter our field of consciousness. This must be made more concrete.

A little reflection shows that in our everyday experience of the world, consciousness is selective. As I listen to a lecture in philosophy much of what is in my visual field fades into unreality as my attention is focused on the speaker, or more particularly on what he is saying. The color of his sport jacket, the texture of the wall behind him, the size of the podium, are "there" just as truly as are the words he is speaking, but they are no part of the world I am now living in. No doubt they could become the center of my attention through a shift of interest, but the point is that the content of experience at any moment is constituted by what I attend to, what interests me. I carve out of the multitudinous data with which I am presented those which shall make up my world. The world that I know is not the total assemblage of what is "there," but those things in the total assemblage which capture my interest. "*My experience,*" says James, "*is what I agree to attend to.*"[13]

At the more abstract level of the workings of the mind the same situation prevails. The process of conception is teleological through and through, determined by our purposes. When we conceive of the essence of some thing, whatever it may be, there is no conceiving of a *given* essence which constitutes the absolute nature of the thing. Common sense may have it this way, but common sense is wrong in this case, says James. What the essence of any thing is depends on our purpose in conceiving it. "The same property which figures as the essence of a thing on one occasion becomes a very inessential feature upon another."[14] As long as I am writing, I conceive of this paper as a fit receptacle for my script, but should I want to light a fire, its essential property becomes that of being combustible; and should I want to make an airplane to sail across the room the paper falls to a new use and so is seen in a different light with consequent different essential properties.

Should one object that this logic applies only to manufactured items which enter our daily experience primarily in terms of their use, James would disagree. In an enlightening footnote to his discussion of this whole question he uses the following example:

> Readers brought up on Popular Science may think that the molecular structure of things is their real essence in an absolute sense, and that water is H-O-H more deeply and truly than it is a solvent of sugar or a slaker of thirst. Not a whit! It is *all* of these things with equal reality, and the

only reason why *for the chemist* it is H-O-H primarily, and only secondarily the other things, is that *for his purposes of deduction and compendious definition* the H-O-H aspect of it is the most useful one to bear in mind.[15]

For the philosopher who might insist that at least in the case of man we know what his true essence is, that of being a rational animal, James would counter by saying that this is not what man is when considered by the biologist or the economist. Why is a definition wrought by the philosopher any more essential than that of the biologist? He, like the biologist, approaches his subject from a particular perspective which is then reflected in his conception of the essence of the thing conceived.

There is then no absolute essence that we know, just as, more broadly speaking, there is no known reality *in se*. Reality confronting and limiting the human knower there is, but what that reality is for any given knower depends on his angle of interest in dealing with it. "The *that* of it is its own," says James in a provocative chapter in *Pragmatism,* "but the *what* depends on the *which*; and the *which* depends on *us*."[16] The *which* here refers to the perspective into which we cast reality. James sums up this point on the teleological character of our concepts as follows: "The essence of a thing is that one of its properties which is so *important for my interests* that in comparison with it I may neglect the rest."[17]

So James' conception of the knowing process is, from top to bottom, a teleological one. All knowing occurs in the context of interest and this interest is a formative factor in what emerges as the known product. It should also be pointed out that James is saying only that it is *a* formative factor, not the only one. There is a resistant factor as well, which means that our cognitive life has only the flexibility allowed by the objective data confronted.

When one takes this view to mean that we never get to know reality in itself, or "in the unimaginable insipidity of its virgin estate,"[18] to use James' more colorful language, then it seems to run counter to our common sense convictions, and to have the heretical ring to it. But looked at in a more positive light, it is the doctrine that reality overflows our perceptions or conceptions of it at every turn. Its richness is such that there is always more to be said about it, always an unexpressed viewpoint. We need take no single account of reality as the definitive account. Any account of it rests on the desire that we have to explain it in accordance with some interest that we may have. There is no telling ahead of time which interests may prove themselves compatible with the reality we confront. The scientific interest has certainly been thus compatible. Perhaps our interest in conceiving the world theistically will turn out likewise.

With this background in mind, let us turn to the reasons James offers for belief in God.

NEED AS A REASON FOR BELIEF

In response to a questionnaire sent out by Professor James Pratt in 1904, James answered a question on why he believed in God by asserting bluntly that he did so because of his need for God.[19] Twenty years earlier, in a letter to Thomas Davidson, James had expressed the same sentiment: "I simply refuse to accept the notion of there being *no* purpose in the objective world," identifying in this context purpose with the existence of God.[20]

At first glance, such assertions seem startling in the extreme coming from a professional philosopher. He is supposed to be the champion of truths based on solid intellectual evidence, not on needs or biases. But from what we have already seen of James' philosophy, we know the central role he assigns to interest and desire in our mental life. Viewed in this context, his statements are not surprising. The business of the ensuing considerations will be to show that these statements accurately reflect the grounds on which James defends religious belief. And I shall further argue that his position is not nearly so soft as it first appears. A start in that direction has already been made in the previous analysis of the role James assigns to the will in our cognitive life. This shall be related to the present issue.

In considering earlier the importance of religious belief, a central point was how belief served to support the strenuous mood. Man wants his actions to have a significance of a deep and lasting sort. This significance is not realized in the materialistic outlook, where "All is vanity" is the final word which the world speaks to man. We argued that the perspective of ultimacy in which this argument is cast could be appreciated through looking at the background experiences of James' own life.

These considerations are important in regard to the present issue because they show the character of the need which James has in mind when he speaks of believing in God because of the need to do so. In the same questionnaire, James asserts that he conceives of God as a "more powerful ally of my own ideals."[21] This is exactly the God of the strenuous mood, the God who supports one's efforts and gives one's ideals a deeper meaning. Given this framework, what happens if there is no God? What happens is that man's life is drastically diminished. It loses the essential support that enables it to realize its deeply human character, to exist in the strenuous mood. So when James speaks of believing in God because he needs Him, the need he is talking about is no superficial, whimsical, erasable human need. It is a need affirmed out of the deepest reserves of the human person. "This need of an eternal moral order is one of the deepest needs of our breast," says James, affirming a point that became clear in the discussion of the importance of religion.[22]

If we realize what is at stake in the question of God's existence, that is, if we recognize the deep-seated need that James is speaking of when he says he believes in God because he needs Him, then his position becomes a very persuasive one. The question came to him in this form: affirm God or accept the absurdity of life. This question is the basic one about what meaning life shall have. If the deepest needs of man are not met by the world in which he finds himself, then life is absurd. In that case, in matters that are of greatest importance, frustration is the final word. There are philosophers who accept that conclusion and who even draw out of it man's dignity as defiantly accepting the absurdity of his situation. James did not do this. Instead, he affirmed life in its fullness. Putting the matter in this context enables us to see that when James speaks of need as the reason for his belief in God, he is simply affirming the fundamental worth of life.

Stating the matter thus is not stating it too strongly. If one sees life in the perspective of ultimacy, as James or any other religious person does, then to deny God is to deny human life. At the truly important level the wants of man are unfulfilled. To deny in principle the possibility of basic human needs being fulfilled is the definition of an absurd world. It might be true that the values that can be realized on a day-to-day basis in our lives, without any reference to God, are enough to make life worth living in some sense. James would not deny that. But the point remains that the religious person interprets life as standing in need of deeper grounding than that afforded by naturalism, and if this need is not met, then our existence is lacking at its most vital point. Life may not lose all meaning because of this, but it is radically diminished. The alternative is to affirm life through affirming God, as James did. If one denies that religious belief has a crucial function in human life, then, of course, the conclusion about absurdity does not follow. But to do this one would have to show that the argument of the previous chapter was lacking.

A further point should be made regarding the logic of belief based on need. As James conceives it, such belief is a matter of allowing the self to follow its natural leaning toward life-supporting beliefs. He is not encouraging an artificial adoption of some belief that is foreign to the person. The total self, emotional and intellectual, inclines one toward the acceptance of this belief in the worth of life. The question becomes one of whether the person should allow himself to be pushed away from that toward which he is deeply inclined, or whether he should allow the weight of his total existence to follow its natural path. Too often James has been interpreted as encouraging beliefs that have no stronger basis in the self than a simple act of will exercised on any want we may have. This is not the case in the matter we are considering. This point will be taken up more fully in our discussion of "The Will to Believe."

Relating our present consideration on need as a basis for belief to that of the previous section on the volitional basis of science, a few points should be made explicit. It is to be expected that a philosophy which finds a volitional basis even in science would argue that need should have its say in religious matters as well. As we have seen, James, in keeping with his notion of the mind as an interested and selective agency, affirms that the enterprise of science is rooted in the human desire to cast the world into a rational shape that it does not have in its everyday garb. The fundamental postulate —unproven, unprovable, but accepted—that underlies science is the uniformity of nature. The scientist necessarily presupposes in his search after underlying connections that there are such connections, that nature is intelligible in the form demanded by the scientific inquiry. James delights in pointing out that this postulate of science is as much a demand on our part as is the moral demand that our endeavors have lasting significance, or that our wills be free.

> The principle of causality, for example,—what is it but a postulate, an empty name covering simply a demand that the sequence of events shall some day manifest a deeper kind of belonging of one thing with another than the mere

arbitrary juxtaposition which now phenomenally appears? It is as much an altar to an unknown god as the one that Saint Paul found at Athens. All our scientific and philosophic ideals are altars to unknown gods. Uniformity is as much as is free-will.[23]

If there is this demand at the heart of our efforts to conceive of the world scientifically, why should it be allowed in this case but not in the moral or religious one? Both demands are equally subjective and equally basic.

James points out elsewhere that it is only by trying out our "dumb convictions" that they will be either verified or disconfirmed. The scientist has done that and his progress in discovering more and more causal relationships in nature tends to confirm his original intuition about the uniformity of nature. The theist should do likewise. He must act on his conviction that the universe is deeply moral and that it calls for a particular response on our part. No neat and short-term confirmation is possible in this case. In fact, the life of the human race may be necessary to determine its truth, but James thinks that it should be treated "exactly as does the physical philosopher in testing an hypothesis":

So here: the verification of the theory which you may hold as to the objectively moral character of the world can consist only in this,—that if you proceed to act upon your theory it will be reversed by nothing that later turns up as your action's fruit; it will harmonize so well with the entire drift of experience that the latter will, as it were, adopt it, or at most give it an ampler interpretation without obliging you in any way to change the essence of its formulation. If this be an objectively moral universe, all acts that I make on that assumption, all expectations that I ground on it, will tend more and more to interdigitate with the phenomena already existing.[24]

Cast into this experimental framework, the religious hypothesis deserves testing as much as does any other. To what extent we can realistically speak of tests in this context is a matter to which we shall give our attention shortly.

Implicit in the above discussion about the volitional basis of both science and religion is another point which tends to justify the adoption of religion based on need. For in doing so we are simply accepting the way in which human nature operates anyway. The "whole man" is at work when we postulate continuity in nature. The whole man is at work when different scientists, on the basis of the very same evidence, offer different explanations of a particular phenomenon. Peculiar sensitivities and inarticulated tendencies are operative here. The same is even more manifestly true when it comes to the espousal of different philosophical theories.

> Pretend what we may, the whole man within us is at work when we form our philosophical opinions. Intellect, will, taste, and passion co-operate just as they do in practical affairs; and lucky it is if the passion be not something as petty as a love of personal conquest over the philosopher across the way. The absurd abstraction of an intellect verbally formulating all its evidence and carefully estimating the probability thereof by a vulgar fraction by the size of whose denominator and numerator alone it is swayed, is ideally as inept as it is actually impossible. It is almost incredible that men who are themselves working philosophers should pretend that any philosophy can be, or ever has been, constructed without the help of personal preference, belief, or divination. How have they succeeded in so stultifying their sense for the living facts of human nature as not to perceive that every philosopher, or man of science either, whose initiative counts for anything in the evolution of thought, has taken his stand on a sort of dumb conviction that the truth must lie in one direction rather than another, and a sort of preliminary assurance that his notion can be made to work; and has borne his best fruit in trying to make it work?[25]

So this is how man is. In our efforts to understand and to cope with the world we live in there is much more at work than dispassionate intellectual insight.

Some might want to bemoan the human character described above and work toward reconstituting man as a more purely intellectual creature. James would not be numbered among them. Our "deepest organ of communication with the nature of things," he believes, is the "dumb region of the heart in which we dwell alone with our willingnesses and unwillingnesses, our faiths and fears."[26] This is the way it has always been and such is the way it will continue to be. "This is the character of the cognitive element in all the life we know, and we have no reason to suppose that character will ever change" says James, referring to the teleological nature of the mind.[27] Our wider self provides an instinctive communication with the world, dumbly asserting itself and providing the direction for further probing. This self has certainly proved itself prescient in the case of our scientific endeavors. Why might not the same be the case in our moral ones?

It is necessary, when immersed in James' voluntarism as we have been, to periodically step back and to recall the limited scope that he is urging for the exercise of our volition. He is not suggesting that we believe what is incompatible with our everyday understanding of the world or with established scientific truths. Nor is this voluntarism a matter of accepting beliefs which barely skirt the edge of nonsense. What James does argue for is the right to believe when that belief is basic to the meaning of life and arises out of needs fundamental to man. And as we have seen, his argument seeks to draw strength from showing a kinship between the generating forces of science and religion, with the result that respect cannot be given to one and withheld from the other. This raises a serious question, however, about the closeness of this kinship. It is to that question that we shall now turn.

We have up to this point stressed the fact that science, like philosophy and religion, comes into being through the activity of a mind, which is an interested and selective agency. At the core of science is the postulate of a uniformity in nature, and in the more particular inquiries of the scientist, the mind actively proposes hypotheses and experiments. In all of this James sees the mind as operating under the impetus of will in its desire to discover a rational order not given in immediate experience. Thus, science, at least in its genesis, is a product of will. The same is true for philosophical and religious hypotheses. The person comes to the world with certain demands he wants satisfied, and he proposes them as hypotheses to live by.

But beyond this point we have a sharp difference in the scientific and philosophic enterprises. For science has developed a method for testing particular hypotheses that are proposed, a method universally accepted by those engaged in science. So, while in the scientific realm there may be a voluntaristic element in hypotheses actively proposed by the mind, there is a hardened method for determining the truth of such proposals. The same is not true of religious hypotheses. These too arise out of demands we have, but there are no objective means for determining their truth or falsity. In this case, we are left with the bare assertion of need and no subsequent method for dealing with these demands. In the absence of any such method, the need which gives rise to the religious hypothesis also becomes the arbiter of the truth of that hypothesis. Belief, then, is totally determined by need. In short, the contrast is this: in science, interest and need generate hypotheses, but their truth is determined by objective methods; in religious matters, interest and need generate hypotheses and these very same needs remain the arbiters of their truth.

The contrast described above is basically sound, though it can be softened by a number of considerations. It might be argued that definitive verification does not occur in science or that hypotheses of a general nature may elude verification. And the postulate of a uniformity throughout nature can never be verified. In spite of this, however, there is still an agreed upon method by which hypotheses are tested. We do know how to go about confirming or disconfirming a scientific hypothesis. Regarding the postulate of the uniformity of nature, certainly it can never be formally verified, but the continued success of science in finding further and further causal connections in nature provides a reasonable basis for asserting that this demand is not folly. So, while the credentials of science can be qualified, they remain impressive.

On the philosophic side, it cannot be said that complete capriciousness reigns regarding the acceptability of hypotheses. Canons of rationality of a rigid sort have been developed that are applied by philosophers. The voluntarism of James would be abhorred by most philosophers who see their own position as resting on sound intellectual evidence. And James himself, while spurned by other philosophers for his lenience in matters of belief, never advocated a casual acceptance of philosophical propositions as true. They must not, for example, be contradicted by our sensible experience, nor clash with other propositions we hold true. Obviously, then, philosophers themselves have certainly developed standards of evidence that apply in their realm.

Despite the claim of intellectual rigor, the fact remains that philosophers as a whole have no means of settling their disputes. Names like *rationalist* and *empiricist* testify to this fact. While any philosopher, or any school of philosophy, may apply its tests of truth rigorously enough, the same tests are ignored by other philosophers. Every position involves presuppositions about the intelligibility of reality which meet with resistance from contrary-minded philosophers. It is this circumstance which leads James to proclaim the undignified view that "the history of philosophy is to a great extent that of a certain clash of human temperaments."[28] The philosopher "trusts his temperament. Wanting a universe that suits it, he believes in any representation of the universe that does suit it."[29] While this is an overstatement, the element of truth in it is its recognition that subjectivity does pervade the enterprise of philosophy to an extent not found in science. Issues cannot be resolved on a theoretical basis in philosophy as they can be in science. And so need not only impels inquiry and asserts demands in philosophy, but it also significantly determines what we shall hold as true.

The philosopher's position, then, is certainly a softer one than is that of the scientist when it comes to a question of method. But we must remember that this is only part of the story. Despite its real area of strength, science has been disarmed of any pretension to tell the whole truth about reality insofar as it has been shown to spring from only a partial interest in it. This opens the door to other possible truths. On the other hand, the above considerations do leave the religious proponent walking through that door armed with only his subjective demands. This is far from a negligible credential given James' analysis, but it is one that would certainly welcome support from other quarters. James attempted to provide this support in a number of ways.

The best known way was his defense of the right to believe despite the continued uncertainty of that in which we believe. His essay "The Will to Believe" draws out this position most extensively. But James also tried to secure support for religion by an examination of religious experience. This he does in *The Varieties of Religious Experience*. He argues there that, epistemologically, religious experience is in a stronger position than it is usually given credit for. And he also shows the great power of religion in the lives of its adherents, a matter we have already looked into. This latter consideration takes on further importance in respect to his argument for man's right to believe. We will look first at James' "will to believe" theory and then at his analysis of religious experience as rounding out his justification of religious belief.

THE RELIABILITY OF RELIGIOUS EXPERIENCE

Although James was completely unwilling to accept the dogmatic claims made on behalf of religious experience, he was equally unwilling to dismiss such experiences as merely interesting psychic phenomena with no objective import. In such experiences the person claims to be in touch with a wider reality than is found in ordinary experience, and this claim must be respected. In a letter written to James Leuba in response to a review of *The Varieties of Religious Experience,* James makes this point clearly. Leuba had attempted in his review to explain religious experience in wholly human terms and James, while acknowledging that he himself had had no such experience, countered in behalf of its veridicality as follows:

> Now, although I am devoid of "Gottesbewustsein" in the directer and stronger sense, yet there is *something in me* which *makes response* when I hear utterances from that quarter made by others. I recognize the deeper voice. Something tells me,—*"thither lies truth"*—and I am *sure* it is not old theistic prejudices of infancy.[30]

Although James' sympathies are clear enough from this passage, the justification of his position is not. What he says in *The Varieties* itself will help clarify this latter point.

One of the hallmarks of James' philosophy is its insistence on experience as the ultimate point of justification for any proposed truth. If the deliverances of experience are not accepted in a given case it can only be because the considerations which undermine these deliverances are themselves supported by direct experiences occurring elsewhere. In this case, the latter experiences are accepted at face value. Applied to the claim of religious experience to know some deeper order of reality, this means it should be accepted as such unless it is shown to be in error by appeal to other original experiences. James did not think this had been shown and so he was inclined to accept its basic claims.

In the chapter on "Mysticism" in *The Varieties,* James lays out the various degrees and characteristics of mystical experience, quotes from a large number of accounts of such experiences, and finally asks whether they need to be accepted as authoritative in their claims. The claim that is important for our consideration is the noetic one. Mystical experiences are allegedly "states of insight into the depths of truth unplumbed by the discursive intellect."[31] In his evaluation of such states, James makes three points: (1) that they are and have the right to be absolutely authoritative for those who have them; (2) that those who do not share in this experience need not accept them uncritically; (3) that they break down the authority of non-mystical consciousness to be the sole arbiter of truth.[32]

James' reasoning in support of these points is simple and in keeping with the epistemological point just made. While we all accept our senses as assuring us of certain states of affairs, "mystical experiences are as direct perceptions of fact for those who have them as any sensations ever were for us."[33] It is true that the mystic might place interpretations on his experiences that go beyond their direct deliverances, but the same can be said for our sense experiences. The central point James insists on is that these are direct perceptions of what seems to exist and therefore have a right to be as authoritative as any other direct experience. Those who do not have such experiences, of course, need not uncritically accept them since they have only the account of others to rely on. And this account is by no means uniform in what it reports, and even if it were, it would still only be an appeal to numbers, and thus without logical force.

And, finally, concludes James, the fact of such experiential claims undoes any pretension of our non-mystical consciousness to be the sole dictator of what is real. Mystical states *may* give one access to another realm, providing the "windows through which the mind looks out upon a more extensive and inclusive world."[34] This cannot be disproved. These experiences normally do not contradict the facts of sense experience, but only place them within a more enveloping point of view. One who dogmatizes in his negation of these experiences steps beyond the authority given him by his own experience. He can claim to know what is through his own experience, but he may not claim to know what is not, except insofar as his own experience is contradicted.

The authority of mysticism, however, has most often been attacked via a more indirect route than disputing its truth because it is based on a supposed supersensible intuition. This attack has taken the form of discrediting the experience by showing that it arises out of organic or cultural antecedents that account for this strange state of mind. Pointing out the unusual complex of conditions involved in the genesis of the experience is taken then as a sufficient warrant for ignoring its cognitive claim. This procedure would seem to be in keeping with James' own epistemological framework which allows one to dispute the claims of a given experience by appeal to a theory based ultimately on other direct experiences.

But James does not think this route to the discrediting of religious experience holds up under examination. The very first chapter of *The Varieties* is devoted to refuting it, thereby attempting to forestall objections that were bound to come from that direction. Here again we see James taking account of the scientific challenge to religion, and defusing it to his satisfaction, before moving on to the positive grounds for religious belief. Let us look more closely at how he depicts the challenge to religious experience and why he considers it misguided.

In a critical consideration of religious occurrences, it is important to distinguish two orders of questions: the existential question and the question of value. The first is concerned with the actual facts before us. We can ask of any occurrence what conditions were involved in its coming to be. Such matters as time, place, biographical data, and cultural framework would be relevant here. To take biblical revelation as an example, we can inquire into the personalities of the writers, the understanding of the physical world present in the culture, prevalent literary styles and more. This, in James' terminology, is the existential question, with the focus on the existing conditions under which some event takes place.

The second question is one of value, or "spiritual judgment," as James sometimes calls it. Here we are asking about the worth that some religious event may have, worth as a guide to life or as a source of truth. We may know all there is to know about the existing conditions under which an event came into being, but it is a different question to ask what significance should be assigned to that event. The answer to the one question is not an answer to the other. The latter is the value question. One may, of course, answer the value question in a way that connects it directly with the existential question. Thus, one might say that a religious event that occurs under such and such conditions has no truth value. Take again, for an example, the case of biblical revelation. Some have said that any divine message to mankind is trustworthy only if it occurs under conditions which are not entangled with the personal and cultural limitations of the scriptural writers. But to make such a value judgment does not logically follow from a mere knowledge of existential conditions; it is to make a new judgment about the importance, the significance, of those conditions in their bearing on the question of truth or value.

These distinctions and connections are important in considering the matter of religious experience. For the issue here is whether the value of religious experience can be dismissed through a simple examination of the existing conditions under which it arose, in this case basically conditions of an organic or psychological sort. James calls the theory which attempts to discredit religious experience in this way, "medical materialism." It "finishes up Saint Paul by calling his vision on the road to Damascus a discharging lesion of the occipital cortex, he being an epileptic. It snuffs out Saint Teresa as an hysteric, Saint Francis of Assisi as an hereditary degenerate."[35] According to this theory, the spiritual authority of these persons is undermined once certain existential conditions are uncovered.

James considers this theory far too simpleminded. For one thing, it is based on the acceptance of the psychological hypothesis that the dependence of mental states upon bodily conditions is total. As a methodological postulate this may be valid, but as a metaphysical assertion it is unproven. The greater difficulty, however, lies elsewhere. Even if we grant such a dependence how does it, of itself, determine spiritual significance? Our ordinary tests of truth are not related to the constitution of he who makes an assertion. Even when we speak disparagingly of "feverish fancies" certainly "the fever-process as such is not the grounds of our disesteem—for aught we know to the contrary, 103° or 104° Fahrenheit might be a much more favorable temperature for truths to germinate and sprout in, than the more ordinary blood heat of 97 or 98 degrees."[36] The real reason for the rejection lies in the fact that such assertions cannot hold up under the scrutiny of the convalescent hour.

Continuing further along this line, we can say that, if religious states of mind are dependent upon certain bodily conditions, so would there be a similar dependence for those states of mind involved in the establishing of scientific truths. Yet no one dismisses the truths of scientific assertions because of the organic conditions of their proponents. Nor is that turn of mind which eventuates in the atheist free from its own organic antecedents. When we judge the truth of a scientific theory we do so by criteria quite other than the organic or psychological conditions of the scientist. These theories are tested by logic and experiment. Similar treatment then should be accorded to assertions arising out of religious experiences.

James proposes that the criteria we should use for judging the deliverances of religious experience are "immediate luminousness," "philosophical reasonableness," and "moral helpfulness."[37] These are not criteria of truth manufactured especially for the occasion, but appear repeatedly in James' philosophy. They refer respectively to the directness of the perception involved, its congruence or lack thereof with other truths we hold, and the acceptability of the experience in terms of its relationship to our moral will. Regarding this latter point, James, as we have seen earlier, sees man's will pressing in the direction of life conceived along lines that will satisfy its basic needs. But, as the other criteria testify, this is not done at the expense of fact, or of contradicting other truths we hold. This point will be explored further in a later chapter.

The net result of these considerations is that religious experience must be given a respectful hearing relative to its contention of relating man to a deeper spiritual world. It cannot be dismissed simply because it traverses a different route than ordinary consciousness, nor does the argument based on the antecedent conditions of its experience prove fatal to it. It may be a valid link with the supernatural. As James says in his verdict on mysticism, it breaks down the claim of ordinary consciousness to be the sole determiner of the real.

The attractiveness of religious experience for James lay precisely in the fact that it was experience. It therefore constitutes a concrete, and possibly persuasive, path to the Deity. It escapes the abstractness of argumentation, moving as it does in the deeper grooves of the human subject. These grooves are thicker and more opaque than the luminous world of the intellect, but they are also the real depths out of which man lives his life. This is what interests James. In making a final assessment of the support which religious experience gives to the reality of the Divine, we can do no better than to quote James' own words.

> The whole drift of my education goes to persuade me that the world of our present consciousness is only one out of many worlds of consciousness that exist, and that those other worlds must contain experiences which have a meaning for our life also; and that although in the main their experiences and those of this world keep discrete, yet the two become continuous at certain points, and higher energies filter in. By being faithful in my poor measure to this overbelief, I seem to myself to keep more sane and true. I *can,* of course, put myself into the sectarian scientist's attitude, and imagine vividly that the world of sensations and of scientific laws and objects may be all. But whenever I do this, I hear that inward monitor of which W. K. Clifford once wrote, whispering the word "bosh!" Humbug is humbug, even though it bears the scientific name, and the total expression of human experience, as I view it objectively, invincibly urges me beyond the narrow "scientific" bounds. Assuredly, the real world is of a different temperament,— more intricately built, than physical science allows.[38]

This verdict is far from dogmatic but it does show that in James' mind religious experience lends further credibility to the Divine than it would have if accepted on need alone. The life of religion as a whole cannot be easily dismissed, and combines with our own needs to move us in the direction of belief.

While the above considerations focus on the reliability of religious experience as supporting belief in God, that is not the primary topic of *The Varieties.* Rather it is the importance of religion in the lives of its adherents that is of most interest to James. Religion does something for the individual. It has power, and in its fruits for human life lies its impressiveness. James adverts often to this. For example, in his chapter on "Saintliness" he writes:

> The man who lives in his religious centre of personal energy, and is actuated by spiritual enthusiasms, differs from his previous carnal self in perfectly definite ways. The new ardor which burns in his breast consumes in its glow the lower "noes" which formerly beset him, and keeps him immune against infection from the entire groveling portion of his nature. Magnanimities once impossible are now easy; paltry conventionalities and mean incentives once tyrannical hold no sway. The stone wall inside of him has fallen and the hardness in his heart has broken down.[39]

Similar comments are frequent in *The Varieties*.

The usual reaction to this, of course, is: "All right, religious conviction does have such power in people's lives, but the more fundamental question is whether such conviction has sufficient supporting evidence. If not, then people's lives are built on sand and deserve no merit." Undoubtedly, concentration on the human fruits of religion rightly gives rise to suspicion about the integrity of the belief being considered. James was accused of believing in belief rather than giving due attention to the truth of belief. The previous considerations in this chapter have attempted to blunt this challenge to some extent. James' philosophy overall counters this accusation in a number of other ways, the most controversial of which is the identification of the true and the good in his pragmatic theory of truth. But for the present I would like to relate the importance of belief to another controversial aspect of James' philosophy, his advocacy of the right to believe in the absence of compelling intellectual evidence. One of the conditions for the exercise of this right is that the issue be a momentous one. The account as narrated in *The Varieties* of what religion can do for life establishes religion as of momentous import.

Before moving explicitly into a consideration of "The Will

to Believe" let me, by way of summary, situate it more explicitly in our account of James' justification of belief in God. As we saw, it is need which is the basic force behind religious belief, just as it is in the rest of our conscious life. But as we also saw, religion has no agreed upon means of verification, as does science. Thus, it remains in an intellectually precarious condition. Religious experience lends some support to the credibility of belief, but to the objective observer plausibility is the most favorable verdict possible. What then should be said about the integrity of believing? Do we have a right to believe what is plausible but still objectively uncertain? Or should belief await definitive evidence? James argued against the latter. He defended the right to believe that which was intellectually uncertain, when certain conditions are met. He also argued that those conditions were met in the case of religious belief. "The Will to Believe" lays out the particulars of this argument.

"THE WILL TO BELIEVE"

In light of what we have seen thus far of James' philosophy, it is entirely expected that we should find him writing an essay entitled "The Will to Believe." For his philosophy is pervaded by a sense of the will as a dominating force in the shaping of our convictions. We have seen that he defends need as a reason for belief in God. And this is only one aspect of a wider outlook that embraces our entire conscious life as being under the dominion of will. So when James wrote "The Will to Believe" he was simply elaborating in explicit form certain existing strains in his philosophy, and logically tightening them. Yet the appearance of this essay evoked a sharply negative reaction, as James was accused of advocating a wantonness of belief that licensed unfounded convictions of every sort. For his part James insisted that the essay had been widely misread, that what he really was doing was spelling out the conditions under which beliefs which are objectively uncertain can still be rightfully held.

The major thesis of "The Will to Believe" James states as follows:

> *Our passional nature not only lawfully may, but must, decide an option between propositions, whenever it is a genuine option that cannot by its nature be decided on intellectual grounds; for to say, under such circumstances, "Do not decide, but leave the question open," is itself a passional decision,—just like deciding yes or no—and is attended with the same risk of losing truth.*[40]

The key terms in this thesis, and the reasons James gives in support of it, need explanation.

By "passional nature" he means not simply deliberate volitions but those inarticulate tendencies in each of us that move us toward one belief or another. Basic factors in our psychological makeup and our cultural and intellectual background would be the ingredients going into the formation of this passional nature. James speaks of "fear and hope, prejudice and passion, imitation and partisanship, the circumpressure of our caste and set" as factors shaping our believing tendencies.[41]

By a genuine option James means one that is living, forced and momentous. A living option involves two alternative hypotheses proposed for our belief, each of which makes some appeal to us, however small. For many today, the choice between belief in God or acceptance of atheism is a live option. Each alternative presents itself in a favorable light from some point of view, and thus makes some appeal. A forced option is one wherein the alternatives are unavoidable. "Either read this book or don't" involves a forced option since there is no other alternative; the same is true of the option "Either reap the peculiar benefits of reading this book or go without them."

On the other hand, "Either agree with my thesis or reject it" is not a forced option since one might do neither. A momentous option is one wherein the stakes are large, so that one will lose or gain significantly from the choice which is made. We have already seen that religion is a case of a momentous option.

James is proposing, then, that in the case of genuine options—those that are living, forced and momentous—we are justified in following our passional nature toward the adoption of a belief, despite the fact that there is no decisive intellectual evidence to support that belief. What are his reasons for this position?

To prohibit belief in the case of genuine options is to adopt a rule of belief which insists on the negative duty of caution against error and prohibits the possibility of reaching the truth (and possibly realizing certain benefits) if truth lies on the affirmative side. For if we may accept and act upon established truths only, there follow results which are unjustifiably deprivatory to human life. We are told that scepticism is the only moral position to take in the case of uncertainties, but the option we are dealing with is a forced one. The alternatives are exclusive; there is no middle ground. In such a case scepticism regarding a particular belief is the equivalent of rejecting it. Now if there are benefits to be gained for oneself and others by accepting and living as if some uncertain assertion is true, why must we intellectually and practically proceed as if it is not true? By what logic must we be compelled to accept that side of the assertion that entails a loss for us? Is the commandment to be on guard against error, with a consequent loss of good, more imperative than the duty of taking a chance on realizing the truth with its beneficial consequences? It seems illogical to say that it is. But if one still insists that it is our duty to refrain from belief except where that belief is certain, then at least it should be recognized that this itself is a decision stemming from the passional nature within the person, that same nature which is being condemned in other contexts. For to urge such restraint in belief is itself a moral position, not one based on pure intellectual insight.

All this is somewhat abstract; it needs to be brought down to cases and to have its assumptions spelled out. One important point to note is that, for James, belief is the basis of action. What we believe determines how we shall act. If our actions were no different having accepted the religious hypothesis than they would be without it, then the whole issue becomes trivial and not worth arguing. James is not concerned, as is Pascal in his famous wager, that the price of unbelief is eternal damnation. Instead, he is concerned that sources of energy and action in the world will be cut off if belief is unjustifiably curtailed. So, for example, according to James' opponents, if we are uncertain as to whether or not human nature is basically good we ought not to act as if it is. Consequently, whatever good might result from such a course of action and whatever possible verification of its truth might occur are rendered impossible. What happens if we apply the ban on belief to James' own religious outlook? We have seen that for him the importance of belief in God lay in its relationship to the strenuous mood. For a person to sustain himself in this mood, belief in an eternal moral order is necessary. If such a belief is forbidden, the fruits for oneself and others of acting out of such belief are also lost. This is a loss of considerable importance. Why must mankind be thus deprived when we are no more certain about the lack of such a moral order than we are about its reality? Certainly it was in this binding way that James saw the issue in relationship to his own personal situation, and that is why he championed the right to believe though objective certainty is lacking.

James also brings forth other considerations for justifying belief. Speaking specifically of religious belief he asks, since theism conceives of the world personally, if it is reasonable to expect conclusive proof? In our dealings with other persons it is often our own willing initiative that allows us to make their acquaintance. Their response to us is dependent upon our making a move. Might not the same situation hold in the relationship of man to God?

> We feel, too, as if the appeal of religion to us were made to our own active good-will, as if evidence might be forever withheld from us unless we met the hypothesis halfway. To take a trivial illustration: just as a man who in a company of gentlemen made no advances, asked a warrant for every concession, and believed no one's word without proof, would cut himself off by such churlishness from all social rewards that a more trusting spirit would earn,—so here, one who should shut himself up in snarling logicality and try to make the gods extort his recognition willy-nilly, or not get it at all, might cut himself off forever from his only opportunity of making the gods' acquaintance.[42]

Similar considerations have been put forth by theologians recently who suggest that we should not expect God to reveal himself to man in some logically coercive way, but that the essence of the religious situation is that man freely respond to God's grace.[43]

James' thesis in "The Will to Believe" has been subject to heavy and persistent criticism. A consideration of a few major points of this criticism can help to further clarify his thesis. It has been argued that the faith James is talking about is no religious faith. Instead, it is a calculating, deliberative type of faith, lacking any sense of the presence of God, and simply designed as a form of self-insurance for the believer. In addition, a belief willed into being in this fashion is not even psychologically possible. James' will to believe was parodied as "the will to make-believe" by unsympathetic readers. Also, it has been argued that James justifies too much in this essay. He sanctions belief in anything one would like to believe in, just so it falls within the realm of the possible. I do not think that these points of criticism show an adequate understanding of James' position.

The first point of criticism, that of the nonreligious character of this faith, rests on the assumption that it is not rooted in any truly religious sense or source in the person. In so doing this criticism does not adequately take into account the fact that James is defending the right to believe, and is not talking about a faith brought into being through any sheer act of willing. He does say explicitly in the first paragraph of his essay that it is "a defence of our right to adopt a believing attitude in religious matters."[44] Shortly after its publication he expressed regret at not entitling it "The Right to Believe." If the "will to believe" is understood as a means of generating belief when there is no real inclination thereto, then surely such belief lacks any religious character, and self-insurance would seem to be its only motive. If, however, James' argument is understood as justifying belief, not generating it, then the belief he is talking about need not be seen as the simple product of a deliberative and calculating will. Instead, it becomes a belief toward which we are inclined by the deeper forces of our being, and the question becomes whether we should *refrain* from such belief because of its objective uncertainty.

This is an important point. When the weight of the total self, formed by that variety of factors that makes each of us the complex being we are, leans heavily in the direction of some particular belief, should our believing tendencies be curtailed? As we saw, James argued it should not, but the point relevant to our present consideration is the kind of faith that he is arguing for. It can certainly be considered a religious faith since it issues from religious tendencies in man and not from motives of self-insurance. It is hardly calculating and deliberative since it wants only to be allowed to follow its basic inclinations. There is no make-believe about it, since it is not a matter of believing what you know isn't true. Instead, it is a matter of accepting and acting on what you are deeply inclined to believe, though you know its truth is not certain. Finally, it is psychologically possible to believe in this way. A belief may be subject to recurrent doubts, but the strength of one's believing tendencies may still enable one to accept that belief and to act on it.

Even if we grant that these considerations make James' essay more persuasive, can it not still be argued that in fact he justifies too much? Is not any haphazardly adopted belief covered by his argument? James himself worried about this interpretation of his thesis and spoke to it at the very end of his essay. If we apply the freedom to believe, he says, to some patent superstition, we naturally recoil at the thought of justifying such an unworthy creature. But we need not fear this. It is not possible for an individual to believe what is regarded with such suspicion anyway. "*In concreto*, the freedom to believe can only cover living options which the intellect of the individual cannot by itself resolve. . . ."[45] So while the right to believe may theoretically seem to cover too much, practically speaking it is only possible to exercise it in regard to living options, those toward which our believing tendencies incline us. True, what is a live option for one person may not be so for the next, but here toleration is of the essence. If we are allowed to follow our believing tendencies toward the God of Christianity, certainly the Hindu must be allowed as much in respect to his God. But this is no matter of concern: concern would be called for if James were read as encouraging or justifying belief in what the person himself considers unbelievable. He did not do that.

Still another point worth noting is that the will to believe is not an invitation to intellectual lethargy. It seeks only to justify belief in the absence of decisive intellectual evidence. It does not tell us to stop looking for such evidence. True, it encourages us not to be so concerned with the possibility that our belief may be false that we are rendered incapable of acting on the possibility that it may be true. But this does not mean that a reconsideration of our beliefs should not, or cannot, take place. In time, what we presently believe may grow incredible for us as new evidence appears, or as available evidence takes on new meaning for us. For example, some persons who once accepted the theory of free will have come to reject it as psychology has progressed in its knowledge of the bodily conditions involved in mental states. Others may hold to the existence of a providential God despite the evil in the world, until one day a personal confrontation with a particularly difficult case of suffering may undo that belief. Thus, new beliefs are adopted, though their evidence may not be decisive either. These persons have remained open to new possibilities through a willingness to re-evaluate the available evidence. We do grow intellectually as individuals and as a culture and in so doing certain beliefs may lose their credibility. We are as much shaped by intellectual considerations as we are by the other facets of our nature. So again James is not suggesting that we stop thinking and start believing, but only that belief need not always wait upon a final verdict from the intellect.

Despite the preceding considerations, it is still difficult to shake off the almost instinctive suspicion aroused by "The Will to Believe." As James suggested, these suspicions are probably sustained by a fear that somehow every half-baked belief has now been justified. He did attempt to overcome this problem, as we saw, through restricting his discussion to live options. Maybe this does not secure the lid tightly enough against loosely accepted beliefs. But even if it does not, this means only that stricter criteria must be developed so as to rule out such beliefs. It does not mean that no belief rightfully falls under the justification James offers.

Further sources of suspicion concern the question of honesty. Isn't there something dishonest about gaining the benefits of living a belief which you know might not be true? Isn't it more in keeping with our dignity as human beings to accept only what we know to be true, whatever the consequent losses are? And again, can we honestly say we believe, and not just pretend to believe, when we know something is intellectually uncertain? Much of what has been said above should help blunt this criticism and the following considerations may be of further help.

It is a fact that when people begin to get more reflective about their lives they are already steeped in beliefs gained through the normal channels of their culture. Such beliefs come to be challenged by exposure to a more diversified environment. Part of this environment may be made up of intellectual considerations which are at odds with these beliefs. In the face of this intellectual challenge what must we do? Must we abandon these beliefs because we may never again be certain of their truth? What if a good part of the meaning of our lives is tied up with those beliefs, and those beliefs entail consequent attitudes and patterns of action? Must these attitudes and patterns of action be abandoned because they no longer rest on certain grounds? Or do we have the right to continue to believe in this case? It seems a harsh and unrealistic doctrine to say that whenever a belief we hold slips into the realm of the intellectually uncertain it must be erased from our lives. Should James have ceased to live in the strenuous mood and clipped his moral wings because he was intellectually uncertain of God's existence? In the case of a forced option, to do that would be to live as if the opposite were true, and that makes no sense.

Obviously, the challenges to our beliefs may sometimes reach the point where we are no longer able to maintain them. And then we abandon them. But not every challenge reaches this point or remains there if it does, despite the fact that it may not be able to be decisively refuted. And in these cases we continue to believe and rightfully so. Our lives may be invested in certain beliefs and that investment need not be withdrawn because its status is no longer intellectually certain.

Looked at in this light the will to believe appears as no artificial and dishonest affair. It is not concerned with beliefs that we pick out of the blue, but instead with those that are organic parts of the self. In this form it is practiced by even its most vehement detractors and then, James would say, in that very act of detraction. For what is the insistence on restricting beliefs to the intellectually certain but a desire or demand on their part for a particular form of certainty before a belief may be acted upon?

This leads to yet another consideration which James saw as lending support to his thesis. That is the point, referred to in the previous chapter, that so many of our beliefs are, in fact, held without strictly intellectual considerations providing adequate support. In the early part of "The Will to Believe" James remarks that

> Here in this room, we all of us believe in molecules and the conservation of energy, in democracy and necessary progress, in Protestant Christianity and the duty of fighting for "the doctrine of the immortal Monroe," all for no reason worthy of the name. We see into these matters with no more inner clearness, and probably with much less, than any disbeliever in them might possess.[46]

And it is not simply these secondhand beliefs that are held on this basis. James, as we saw, understands the conflicting philosophies of the world as themselves being rooted in inarticulated preferences that make one or the other position seem like pure reason to its proponent. The logical positivist who declares all metaphysical propositions to be meaningless because they cannot be verified in the way that scientific assertions can is ultimately expressing a desire to have a single sort of intelligibility to decide all questions. The metaphysician who can tie all the logical ends of the world together in his conceptual web is likewise making assumptions about the intelligibility of reality that the more empirical-minded philosopher cannot accept. Thus, at the source of these philosophical positions is the demand, or a deep-rooted preference, that the world shall be of this sort or that. The world is full of different faiths, whether their adherents are aware of this or not. James, of course, is not decrying this situation so long as these faiths are intellectually responsible. But he does count it as a point in his favor that the creeds by which men do live are not simple matters of the intellect. And so while others may argue against his advocacy of faith, they do not themselves live on any other basis. Might we not be better off to recognize what is inescapable and work toward a formulation of a theory for its responsible exercise?

Another consideration which was also previously discussed should be brought to bear on the present issue. It is that the route of faith, responsibly carried out, need not be considered an inadequate way of understanding the world we live in. We saw that James considers man's powers of knowing reality to be wider than those exercised by the intellect alone. He suggests that "to the end of time our powers of moral and volitional response to the nature of things will be the deepest organ of communication therewith we shall ever possess."[47] This deeper region of the self he refers to in another place as the "crepuscular depths of personality" indicating thereby that it involves the total person.[48] We find this deeper but inarticulate region of the self operative in such phenomena as the acceptance of the unproved postulates underlying science or in the divination involved in its discovery of new truths. Given James' acceptance of a wider access to reality than through the intellect alone, it is consistent that he should give the whole self a freer role in the determination of belief. None of this, however, should be construed as the abandonment of the intellect on his part. But it certainly means that its powers should be complemented by those of the more inclusive self.

As a final consideration of "The Will to Believe" let us look at James' own struggle with the question of free will. We have here a clear case of the exercise of the will to believe as it occurred in the life of its proponent. In 1869, he tells us, he was "swamped in empirical philosophy" and found that he was unable to shake himself loose from the grip of determinism. "I feel that we are Nature through and through, that we are wholly conditioned, that not a wiggle of our will happens save as a result of physical laws. . . ."[49] The debilitating implications of this doctrine left James a captive of it, rather than its happy advocate. A reading of Renouvier enabled him to escape its clutches—though, as the following passage shows, not through any definitive disproof of determinism.

> I think that yesterday was a crisis in my life. I finished the first part of Renouvier's second "Essais" and see no reason why his definition of Free Will—"the sustaining of thought *because I choose to* when I might have other thoughts"— need be the definition of an illusion. At any rate, I will assume for the present—until next year—that it is no illusion. My first act of free will shall be to believe in free will.[50]

This passage is as much significant for the intellectual element involved in James turning from determinism as it is for the element of will. James was unable to believe until the doctrine of free will had become intellectually acceptable.

Years later James wrote an essay entitled "The Dilemma of Determinism," in which he drew out the moral implications of determinism and rejected it on the grounds of those implications. Though written more than a decade earlier than "The Will to Believe," this essay worked within the framework of the later essay in rejecting determinism. The issue is one that cannot be decided on intellectual grounds. Yet we may assume it is true and act accordingly.

> I thus disclaim openly on the threshold all pretension to
> prove to you that freedom of the will is true. The most I
> hope is to induce some of you to follow my own example in
> assuming it true, and acting as if it were true.[51]

James goes on to add that our theories about the world are
undertaken "in order to attain a conception of things which
shall give us subjective satisfaction" and that a conception
which, on the whole, is more rational we may suppose to be
the truer.[52] He then points out how determinism, properly
understood, violates our deepest moral demands, and he
accordingly rejects it.

Here James is exercising his right to believe. The matter is
intellectually uncertain. It is an issue which ties deeply into
his moral nature. He accepts and acts on indeterminism while
recognizing its uncertainty. Overall, the issue is related to his
voluntarism which maintains that all theorizing is undertaken
out of the need to satisfy demand. So when James wrote "The
Will to Believe" it was a reflection of what had occurred in his
own life. Thus it was certainly possible, and, as he argued,
also justifiable.

We have spent considerable time on "The Will to Believe"
because it was, and continues to be, a controversial essay, but
mainly because it embodies in explicit form the voluntarism
which is at the heart of James' religious philosophy.

Before turning away from James' justification of religious
belief one consideration remains. What did he find wrong with
proofs, strictly rational argumentation, for the existence of
God? The will to believe is exercised in the absence of such
evidence but why was the evidence itself found lacking? The
answer to this question shows us another important feature
of James' approach to religious questions.

REJECTION OF ARGUMENTS
FOR THE EXISTENCE OF GOD

James expressed his light regard for the arguments for the
existence of God in a number of his writings, but it was in

The Varieties of Religious Experience, in the chapter entitled "Philosophy," that he gave the topic his most sustained attention. This attention never took the form of a technical discussion of the arguments because James could never take them seriously enough to devote such an analysis to them. For him they were an artificial route to the Deity. They might confirm the conviction of the believer, but they had little or no power over one searching for answers. Reason operates here, he says, as it does in such matters as love and politics. It comes after the fact and is simply used to support what we believe in on quite another basis. That basis is feeling, which here includes dimensions of the self wider than the strictly intellectual.

Feeling, says James, is the deeper source of religion. Without it religion would never have come to be, and religious philosophies would not have arisen out of the resources of reason alone. "I doubt if dispassionate intellectual contemplation of the universe, apart from inner unhappiness and need of deliverance on the one hand and mystical emotions on the other, would ever have resulted in religious philosophies such as we now possess."[53] But even if we grant this contention, might it not be that, while feeling prompts us to seek a religious significance in the universe, still the determination of whether there is such a significance and what form it takes is the proper work of reason? The wider self, or feeling self, may be the initiator of our search for God, but the intellectual self may be the proper means of carrying out this search. In this case the arguments for God's existence would have their role to play.

James is not sympathetic to this view. While not ruling out altogether a role for the intellect in religious matters, he does seek to discredit its effort "to construct religious objects out of the resources of logical reason alone, or of logical reason drawing rigorous inference from non-subjective facts."[54] This certainly would include the ontological argument and any causally based argument, be it from design or contingency. These arguments proceed either by drawing out the implications of our concept of God, or by inferring a cause for certain arrangements in the universe, or for its very existence. Thus, they proceed from an analysis of certain objective data to the existence of God. No heed is paid to the facts of religious experience itself. Reason may draw conclusions which go beyond or contradict our religious feelings without paying attention to the testimony of the real source of religion itself.

James rejects this role for reason. The arguments for God's existence have fallen on evil days since the time of Kant; the design argument was further demolished by Darwin's ideas; but even beyond that, the arguments have never been objectively convincing. Based on reason as they allegedly are, their conclusions lay claim to being universally valid. Yet in fact they have done no better in this respect than the private sphere of feelings. They have created sects and disagreements just as have feelings, and so they are entitled to no superior claim in dealing with religion. As stated above, James asserts that reason operates here after the fact and has no independent power to chart the religious universe in any convincing way.

It is not that reason has no role to play in religious matters. James' only contention is that one should not develop a religious philosophy on the basis of reason alone. What is basic to religion is feeling, experience. The subjective life of man is the source of religion. Whatever place reason has in religion will be exercised in using as basic data for reflection the religious experience of mankind. It can help to formulate the content of religious experience. It can determine the compatibility of these formulations with the data of everyday experience and the results of scientific investigation. It can critically assess the validity of religious experience. In these and other tasks reason will perform a needed function, but this function will always be secondary to feeling as a source of religious belief or theory.

Proponents of natural theology would hardly be satisfied

with James' criticism. While it is difficult to dispute his judgment about the checkered history of the arguments for God's existence, still each proponent seems to find some patched up version of such an argument a model of intellectual luminosity. Not to attack that argument on its own grounds, on the way in which it finds reality intelligible, is to skirt the only issue that interests the theist. The ammunition for such an attack lay in James' theory of knowledge, but he never trained it on the arguments as such. The arguments did not interest him because they had no real power to generate belief. Belief arises out of the deeper regions of the self, where the basic, lived confrontation with the conditions of our existence take place. It is there that the need for God is felt. And out of this felt need emerges the movement toward Him. Arguments for God are intellectual and abstract, involving only the surface self. James was interested in the problem of God as one that had to be solved in a personal way. Arguments for God might be philosophically interesting, or they might involve a nest of conceptions that puts the best of philosophers on his mettle, but they didn't do the job that interested James—which was to provide the means for dealing with the question of belief for he who was seeking for truths by which he might live. Much more empirical considerations, close to the center of lived existence, are necessary for that.

This is not to advocate an irrational belief in God. But what James realized was that the only rational considerations that can lead to belief are those that bear on matters that we participate in with our total selves. Our feelings of contingency, of the need for support in the pursuit of ideals, of obligation, are examples of matters that we feel deeply. If it is these that we reflect upon in our search for God, and if our reflections lead to a conclusion supporting belief in the existence of God, these conclusions will have a power of persuasion lacking in our reasoning about nonsubjective facts. They touch us in a way that these other facts do not since they carry within themselves a sense of what is at stake for us in the issue being considered. It was to these subjective facts that James tried to awaken us in his advocacy of belief.

A SUMMARY AND SOME FINAL COMMENTS

This has been a long and many faceted chapter. A summary of its main points along with some final comments will bring it to conclusion.

For James, the first hurdle that religious belief must overcome is the conflicting interpretation of the world presented by science. Actually, it was not science as such that proved to be the enemy of a religious conception of the universe, but the pretension of some that science was the exclusive source of truth about the world. This positivism, or scientism, James rejected firmly. He saw the scientific conception of reality as arising out of the desire to give an account of reality in particular mathematical and logical terms. This was a legitimate and fruitful interest, but it was only a partial one. Man has other interests that deserve a hearing as well. We have moral and religious interests that seek satisfaction, and these interests have as much right to be tried as do our scientific ones. The fact that the scientific interest has developed a method of verifying hypotheses, and has borne rich fruits as a result, still does not mean that what it has to say about the world is all that can be said. Its account is valid only so far as it goes.

What James emphasized about science was the fact that it was ultimately based on interest and desire. Put in this perspective, it was only a short step to its dethronement and to the establishment of a democracy of interests. True, the glory rightfully belongs to science for developing an objective method for determining its truths. But one must be careful not to confuse the objectivity of the scientific method with the quite different assertion that science offers an objective—in the sense of disinterested—account of the world.

This position on the status of science is simply one application of James' overall view on the teleological character of the human mind. The mind is no passive recorder of the given; it is a creature of interests, actively organizing and conceptualizing the world from various perspectives. Science is only one of those perspectives.

Given James' understanding of interest and need as the basis of our conception of the world, it is not surprising that he affirms his own belief in God based on need. God is needed as a support for the strenuous mood, and He is accepted accordingly. James maintains both that God is, in fact, believed in because we need Him, and that such belief is legitimate. This legitimacy is supported in a number of ways. First, there is, as we have seen, need at the basis of any account of the world. Thus, in terms of source, need here has as much right to assert itself as it does anywhere else. But such an assertion is shaky unless supported by evidence. This leads to the second support, which is that of religious experience. This experience cannot be discounted as a valid source of a wider understanding of the world than we gain through the employment of our everyday ways of knowing. And, finally, even though none of the above considerations are decisive in establishing the truth of religion, we still have the right to believe in the religious hypothesis if it is a genuine one. And it is, so long as religion is a live option for an individual. Thus, these various strands of James' thought come together to vindicate belief in God.

I have argued that the most controversial of these strands, the right-to-believe thesis, deserves a better hearing than it has gotten. Once we realize that James is not justifying the generation of beliefs of an exogenous sort, his argument takes on a new character. The argument instead revolves around the question of whether we must foreswear beliefs toward which we are deeply inclined simply because those beliefs are objectively uncertain. To say that we may live in these beliefs is not to create any make-believe world. It only legitimates what even its opponents practice as they are preaching against it.

So much by way of summary. Some commentators on James' religious philosophy have said that he never really believed in the objective existence of a God, but that he only believed in the right to believe. It is readily understandable that this comment should be made. James did stress, as we have seen, the importance of belief for the strenuous mood and for the sick soul. He did write an entire book, *The Varieties of Religious Experience,* which approached religion from the point of view of what it does in the lives of its adherents. He did write an essay on the right to believe despite uncertainties about the reality of that in which you believe. He did speak of believing because he needed God; and his best-known contribution to philosophy has been the doctrine of pragmatism, which is widely understood as advocating the acceptance of any belief which works, whether or not it is true. Thus it would be grossly contrary to fact to say that there is no basis in James' religious philosophy for interpreting it simply as a belief in believing.

But this is not the whole story. Certainly James did believe in believing; that is the thesis of "The Will to Believe," which is closely tied to his overall philosophical outlook. But he also believed in the reality of God as a power beyond human consciousness. It was the acceptance of the actuality of such a power that enabled James to live in the strenuous mood. If belief in God is necessary to sustain one in the strenuous mood, and if James lived thus, then he believed in God. This is not belief in believing: it is accepting God as a wider power in the universe who confers a dimension of significance upon human endeavors. James believed in that God.

As a thoroughgoing empiricist in philosophy he did not, however, think we could ever reach certitude in these matters. So if doubt and belief are incompatible, then, of course, James never believed. If they are incompatible, then the whole thesis of the will to believe makes no sense, for it urges belief in the face of an objective uncertainty that always leaves doubts. So James certainly accepted their compatibility. Why cannot one accept a particular belief, and live in the light of that belief, while recognizing that this is a matter of faith and that its truth is subject to doubt? Many do this. The factor of doubt does not necessitate that we interpret James as simply believing in believing.

James did assert in his consideration of religious experience that he himself had no living sense of commerce with the Divine. Here he was speaking of the type of communion with God enjoyed by mystics, saints, and the more ordinary religious persons as they experience themselves living in the divine presence. The lack of this religious sense again does not mean a lack of the acceptance of the reality of the Divine. James thought of God as an ally of his ideals and accepted Him as such. One need not feel the presence of this God to affirm His existence. James did express his regret over the lack of any such experience in his own life but this did not deter him from accepting the reality of God.

Nor did he encourage others to believe simply for the sake of believing. True, he did justify belief in the case of genuine options, but this is applicable only to beliefs to which we are organically related. To argue against putting a stopper on our tendencies toward deep-seated beliefs is hardly to encourage one simply to believe in something so as to have something to believe in. As we saw, James did think that belief was also necessary as a means of confirming or ruling out particular hypotheses. This too argues against his encouraging of belief simply for its own sake.

Probably the underlying reason that has led some to interpret James as believing only in belief is the very character of his concern about religion. Had he attempted to develop proofs of God's existence like others did, or had he developed a systematic theology bearing on God's attributes, the question would not have arisen. But James was interested in the

God question as it actually took hold of a person's life. He was interested in those considerations which moved people to believe or which served as stumbling blocks to that belief. So most of his attention was trained on man and the dynamics of his experience. What use to offer proofs for God's existence when they have no power to persuade anyway, and when they leave the man for whom religious belief was a real issue where he was in the first place? This was how James saw the problem, so quite naturally the center of his attention was man. Undeniably, his religious philosophy was interested in enhancing human life. But none of this means that he was not interested in the reality of God. His interest called for approaching God through man so that his reflections would tie into the needs of concrete human beings.

Nor should this be taken as something that only James has done. One need not look far today for theologians who begin their inquiry about God by looking at man. Their first question is what kind of God can man believe in, given his present-day understanding of the physical world and himself. They declare that the God of our forefathers is dead. Only a God who is truly respectful of human autonomy, who does not make on-the-spot incursions into the processes of nature, and who did not in the fullness of his wisdom permit Auschwitz can be believed in today. God must be reinterpreted accordingly. No more than James have these people lost sight of God, but they do consciously operate out of the conviction that, since it is man who is supposed to believe in God, and since his view of God is shaped by what he is, there is little sense in trying to bypass the human component in speaking of God. To do so will render one's treatise immediately sterile so far as relating to the real problem of the religious person is concerned.

This chapter has been an attempt to present James' voluntarism in a perspective that does it greater justice than when it is considered simply in terms of isolated expressions. Be-

lieving because of need or constructing theories for our subjective satisfaction sounds like the abandonment of all intellectual responsibility. It is not, as we have seen.

In addition to working out a justification for religious belief, James also offered some reflections concerning the nature
of God. The next chapter will be a consideration of this aspect
of his thought.

4.

The Nature of God

The God that William James believed in is a finite God. He is not the omnipotent creator of all that is, but, like us, He has obstacles to contend with in His work. Nor is He the timeless and omniscient being of traditional Christianity. Instead, He exists in time, with a range of knowledge consistent with that status. But of greater interest than the particular conception of God that James advocated are the reasons he gave for his position. In his view there are certain values in human life that are incompatible with the existence of an infinite being, and these values are of such importance that in their name such a being must be denied.

The same concerns that led James to affirm the existence of God also shape his conception of God. The primary purpose that the existence of God serves in his philosophy is as a support for the strenuous mood. God is a moral stimulant. If this is why God is needed, then His nature must be so conceived as to allow man a morally stimulating role in the world. James opposes those conceptions of God which he feels deprive man of this role.

There are other reasons as well that influence James' conception of God. He insists that God must be such as to allow for an "intimacy" between God and man. To a large extent this reason is reducible to the previous one, though it is also related to his concern that the Divine will have an efficacious place in man's life, as in religious experience. Finally, the age-old problem of reconciling the evil in the world with an infinite God influenced James. Given again the strenuous character of his universe, he naturally thought it better to leave evil as something that must be actively opposed by all the powers of goodness, rather than to try to show how it is compatible with an omnipotent being who could eradicate it by his mere fiat.

These reasons for the divine finitude are brought out most clearly in James' criticism of the theistic positions he opposes. This criticism will be explored in detail along with the resulting conception of God that James offers. Before doing this, however, a preliminary comment regarding his way of handling this problem is in order. Just as he found no route to God possible that reasoned from objective facts in the world to the divine existence, neither does he find it possible to determine the nature of God in that fashion. We cannot discover God's attributes through any metaphysical insight, nor infer them through any reasoning process built on that basis. Thus, as in the case of the existence of God, James feels free to draw his conclusions based on their compatibility with the religious and moral needs at stake and with other known facts about the world. So if an infinite God is incompatible with man's need for a morally stimulating existence, that God is unacceptable. Stated so bluntly, James' procedure seems to lack the intellectual rigor usually employed by philosophers in dealing with God. In evaluating his position at the end of this chapter, I will return to this issue and argue for the legitimacy of his approach.

As was said above, James' finite God theory emerges out of his criticism of other positions. His theory was formulated against the background of the absolute idealism of his day and the more traditional Christian theism. Each of these views he found deficient in different respects. Considered in relation to their relevance to James' criticism the essentials of these positions can be stated briefly.

Absolute idealism is the theory that the world is the progressive unfolding of the Absolute as world spirit. This process is the temporal or historical dimension of that ultimate reality wherein it is immanent in the world's development. Besides this temporal aspect of the Absolute, there is also its eternal dimension wherein it transcends the world and exists in timeless perfection. In this dimension all that is, was, or will be exists as simultaneously present to the Absolute. This theory is idealistic insofar as reality is conceived of as spirit—as idea: while we can make our ordinary distinction between the mental and the physical, still a oneness prevails insofar as everything is grounded in, and an immanent dimension of, world spirit.

This theory differs sharply from traditional theism insofar as it is pantheistic. Traditionally, God has been thought of as radically distinct from His creation, totally sufficient unto Himself, and unaffected by the world's happenings. He freely chose to create the world. As creator He is causally immanent in it but His being is in no sense that of the world's. Like the Absolute in its eternal dimension, God exists in timeless perfection and is an omniscient Being to whom all is simultaneously present.

With this sketch of the theories James finds deficient let us turn to the particulars of his criticism of them.

CRITICISM OF ABSOLUTE IDEALISM

James offers his most extensive criticism of the Absolute in two of his later works, *Pragmatism* and *A Pluralistic Universe.* In *Pragmatism,* he contrasts the "finite editions" of the world with the "absolute edition" as follows:

Here all is process; that world is timeless. Possibilities ob-
tain in our world; in the absolute world, where all that is
not is from eternity impossible, and all that *is* is necessary,
the category of possibility has no application. In this world
crimes and horrors are regrettable. In that totalized world
regret obtains not, for "the existence of ill in the temporal
order is the very condition of the perfection of the eternal
order."[1]

This characterization of absolutism is suggestive of the age-
old contention that, if the future is infallibly known, even by
a timeless knower, then the future is determined. In recent
philosophical discussion that argument has reached new heights
of sophistication, but in essence it is quite simple.[2]

If what will happen at some future date is infallibly known
today, then that future event cannot be other than what it is
known to be today. That being the case, how can the future
event be called free? There is no possibility of anything else
occurring. A truly free action is one which, at the time of its
occurrence, involves the possibility of an action other than itself occurring. Given the infallible knowledge of what will
occur, however, no other action is really possible. The fact that
this infallible knowledge is said to be timeless, and thus not
knowledge of the future as such, does not relieve the difficulty. For while this knowledge may exist timelessly for the
Absolute knower, the fact remains that what will happen tomorrow is known today, in whatever mode, and therefore that
occurrence and only that occurrence can happen tomorrow.
If then we speak of possibilities, we must realize that we are
speaking only of illusions created by the fact that the finite
creatures of the world do not know what is known, and thus
predetermined, in the Absolute's timeless view of the world.
In reality then, there are no true possibilities.

The defender of the compatibility between a timeless, infallible knowledge and freedom in the world has countermoves
to make to this argument. One of these is the contention that

the argument gains its alleged strength by a failure to recognize the difference between a timeless and a temporal knowledge. A timeless knowledge, as such, is never of the future and hence does not predetermine it as a time-bound vision would. By subtly shifting the meanings of these two notions in the course of the argument, the opponent of the timeless deity applies the logic of a temporal omniscience to the timelessly omniscient Being. He thus draws the false conclusion of the incompatibility between freedom and a timeless omniscience. Along different lines, the defender of the timeless Deity argues that knowledge as such never determines. Thus, even if a God knows infallibly what is going to be, that in itself would not be the determining factor in the occurrence of future events.

James never entered technically into this argument, though he certainly agreed with those who contended that a timeless omniscience entailed determinism.

> A mind to whom all time is simultaneously present must see all things under the form of actuality, or under some form to us unknown. If he thinks certain moments as ambiguous in their content while future, he must simultaneously know how the ambiguity will have been decided when they are past. So that none of his mental judgments can possibly be called hypothetical, and his world is one from which chance is excluded. Is not, however, the timeless mind rather a gratuitous fiction? And is not the notion of eternity being given at a stroke to omniscience only just another way of whacking upon us the block universe, and of denying that possibilities exist?[3]

If there is an omniscient being, then nothing but what he knows can happen. Thus, possibilities in the ordinary sense of the word—alternatives, either of which might actually occur—are ruled out. James' use of the word *chance* in this context should not be misconstrued. He is not talking about a universe of random occurrences, but simply of one wherein different futures can be brought about by human choices.

Even if one grants that James and others are correct in their contention that divine omniscience and human freedom are incompatible, there is no immediate theological problem unless one insists upon the reality and importance of human freedom. This has not always been the case. Jonathan Edwards, for example, in his *Freedom of the Will,* denied human freedom or, more accurately, defined it in such a way as to make it compatible with divine omniscience.[4] He saw the latter as more important than the former. This may be acceptable in a God-centered world where men are more concerned about extolling the merits of the Deity than they are about giving their present life full significance. Such was not the case with James, nor, more generally, is it true of twentieth-century theological thought. Man's temporal concerns have been accorded a place of greater importance as have his responsibilities in pursuing these concerns. Thus, the freedom of man cannot be denied in favor of the power and dominance of God.

On this basis, then, James was ready to deny God's omniscience. He was not, however, so much interested in the technical question of the incompatibility of divine omniscience and human freedom as he was interested in the consequences for human life that followed from a religious orientation centered on the Absolute. If a person sees the universe in relation to the Absolute then he sees it as eternally complete: the Absolute undergirds the world and holds it together in a timeless unity that is without possibilities. To see the world in this fashion is to see it as a two-dimensional affair, composed of the realm of the imperfect and that of the perfect. The world of incomplete and distorted perspectives where men struggle and suffer is a world of imperfect visions and aspirations, inferior to the eternally complete and perfect world of the Absolute. The task of the religious person is to accept the world as thus perfect in this deeper view. The key word here is *accept.* We acquiesce in the given. What happens is accepted as somehow related to the perfection that will ultimately be brought out of the present situation. The religious call essentially is to transcend our present, limited viewpoint so as to see all that is in a deeper light.

James did find a certain value in this outlook, but ultimately he rejected it. It violated the deepest yearning of his moral being. He insisted that our present existence be left with the fullness of meaning it has when not interpreted from a foreign perspective. There must be no viewpoint that is essentially different from our own. Life is a matter of meeting the problems the world presents by transforming it in keeping with the values we hold. The world is the realm of real possibilities that calls upon us to work for its betterment. The outcome is not yet known or assured. What is happening here and now, what efforts we exert, will determine the outcome.

When we come then to speak about God, we should not think of that God as existing in an order of reality, or with a viewpoint, essentially different from our own. Certainly God is greater than us, a deeper power in the universe, but He is not the inhabitant of a totally different realm, embodying a totally different perspective from our own. Our vision may be considerably less encompassing than that of the Divine, but what is important is that this is a difference of degree, not of kind. The real world, the world of true reality, is the very world that we are in the process of working to better. God is part of that world and not the inhabitant of a foreign domain. Thus the urgency is in no sense drained away from the projects of our present existence by tying it to a realm that encourages us to accept whatever is because it is an element of perfection in a world that transcends our own.

What James, in the passage which was quoted at the beginning of this chapter, says about regret is related to the present point. What real meaning does regret have when, at a deeper level, every regrettable happening is seen as a necessary ingredient in bringing about some further good. Truly, that event is not regrettable, but only appears so to one whose insight is too partial to see things from the deeper perspective. Such a view saps our everyday life of its full meaning. If, on the contrary, there is no other dimension radically different from our own, then these events are regrettable, just as they appear to be. The challenge in this case is to do something about the world in which regrettable events occur rather than to point out their goodness as seen from the point of view of the Absolute.

Thus, the Absolute would deprive the world we live in of its reality in the form in which that reality is taken in ordinary experience. James calls it the great de-realizer of life. If we erase the Absolute we give to our life as ordinarily perceived the fullness of meaning. That life is one that is morally stimulating. The deepest meaning of our lives comes from the fact that we are important determinants of what shall be.

The challenging character of the world James envisions is brought out nicely in the following passage.

> Suppose the world's author put the case to you before creation, saying: "I am going to make a world not certain to be saved, a world the perfection of which shall be conditional merely, the condition being that each several agent does its own 'level best.' I offer you the chance of taking part in such a world. Its safety, you see, is unwarranted. It is a real adventure, with real danger, yet it may win through. It is a social scheme of co-operative work genuinely to be done. Will you join the procession? Will you trust yourself and trust the other agents enough to face the risk?"[5]

The major point of the passage is quite simple. The world may be conceived as a place whose future is truly indeterminate. Thus, we are presented with a challenge. The burden is on us to secure a favorable outcome. Each person must do his part. There are no guarantees beforehand. This world is a place of real adventures, real dangers, and real tragedies. As such it calls upon our energies; it stimulates us to make our contributions. Were it, on the contrary, simply the enactment of a cosmic scheme whose ultimate perfection was antecedently guaranteed, and whose various parts, however tragic, were necessary ingredients in bringing about that perfection, those energies would not be required and man's significance would be drastically diminished.

Obviously, this universe is fit only for the healthy minded. The needs of the sick soul are left out. James is not totally happy about this, but consistency demands that a choice be made in this matter. We cannot have both a God who saves us, no matter what, and a world whose salvation truly depends upon what we do. With some misgivings about the needs his theory does not meet, James opts for the healthy-minded alternative.

> In the end it is our faith and not our logic that decides such questions, and I deny the right of any pretended logic to veto my own faith. I find myself willing to take the universe to be really dangerous and adventurous, without therefore backing out and crying "no play." I am willing to think that the prodigal son attitude, open to us as it is in many vicissitudes, is not the right and final attitude towards the whole of life. I am willing that there should be real losses and real losers, and no total preservation of all that is.[6]

Thus, as we saw earlier, in the final analysis, James sees life as lived in the strenuous mood as the more fit alternative.

In *A Pluralistic Universe,* whose very title proclaims it the antithesis of monism or absolutism, James' criticism of the Absolute follows somewhat different lines. Here he initially praises absolutism for providing man with an intimate relationship with the universe. It affords man this intimacy in two respects. First of all, it is a spiritualistic philosophy rather than a materialistic one. As such the ultimate source of reality is not alien to man, but is of the nature of spirit or mind. But more than this it makes man one with the Divine insofar as it falls within "the pantheistic field of vision, the vision of God as the indwelling divine rather than the external creator, and of human life as part and parcel of that deep reality."[7] With the human substance thus identical with the Divine, the basis for a meaningful relationship, a creative exchange between God and man, is secured.

But while this degree of intimacy is achieved in absolutism, there is another factor in that theory that leaves the Divine a foreigner to human concerns. Again it is the timelessness of the Absolute that is the culprit. In this form it is utterly unlike us, existing in a realm removed from that of finite interests and concerns.

> As absolute, then, or "sub specie eternitatis," or "quatenus infinitus est" the world repels our sympathy because it has no history. *As such,* the absolute neither acts nor suffers, nor loves nor hates: it has no needs, desires, or aspirations, no failures or successes, friends or enemies, victories or defeats.[8]

In its deepest reality the world loses touch with all that is familiar to us. As such we cannot enter into a meaningful relationship with it since its mode of experience is totally different from our own.

Why is James so opposed to the Deity being radically unlike man? Most theists have worked hard to secure the transcendence of God, his otherness from man, and have counted this as a virtue of their theory. But James affirmed the opposite. The reason for this lies in the point previously considered: a completely transcendent God cannot serve as a moral stimulus to man. This becomes clear in a later passage.

> But the world that each of us feels most intimately at home with is that of beings with histories that play into our history, whom we can help in their vicissitudes even as they

help us in ours. This satisfaction the absolute denies us; we can neither help nor hinder it, for it stands outside of history. It surely is a merit in a philosophy to make the very life we lead seem real and earnest.[9]

Intimacy here is being thought of in terms of a world that elicits our efforts. The Divine is in history, not outside it. Because this is so there is no dimension of reality that escapes the effect of man's action. The importance of this action is not reduced by its being operative only in a secondary sphere. Reality in its fullness is what man is grappling with in his everyday existence. James affirms here, as he does elsewhere, that the Deity itself may be thought of as needing our help. There are only beings whose histories play into ours, whom "we can help in their vicissitudes even as they help us in ours." If we could not contribute to reality in its deepest form, then again our lives are diminished. James is insistent on a universe that allows for the efficaciousness of man's actions.[10] This vision first of all demands a God so that man's values are anchored deeply in reality, but secondly, and just as importantly, this God must need us just as we need Him in our mutual work. The result is a universe of maximum moral stimulation.

Thus, while James speaks of the desirability of intimacy between God and man, it is not intimacy as such that he seeks. This intimacy is being thought of in terms of its relationship to the morally stimulating world James would like to secure.

A further point of criticism which James directs against the theory of the Absolute stems from the existence of evil in the world. This is the ancient problem of reconciling evil with a perfect being who is the creative source of all that is. James states the difficulty as follows.

It introduces a speculative "problem of evil" namely, and leaves us wondering why the perfection of the absolute should require just such particular hideous forms of life as darken the day for our human imaginations. If they were forced on it by something alien, and to "overcome" them the absolute had still to keep hold of them, we could understand its feeling of triumph, though we, so far as we were ourselves among the elements overcome, could acquiesce but sullenly in the resultant situation, and would never just have chosen it as the most rational one conceivable. But the absolute is represented as being without environment, upon which nothing alien can be forced, and which has spontaneously chosen from within to give itself the spectacle of all that evil rather than a spectacle with less evil in it. Its perfection is represented as the source of things, and yet the first effect of that perfection is the tremendous imperfection of all finite experience.[11]

Monistic theism in every form has had to struggle with this problem, and over the centuries it has been the most persistent and formidable obstacle to belief in God. James does not bring up the most difficult instances of evil, such as the sufferings of innocent children, but focuses instead on the question of how the perfection of the Absolute is enhanced by the creation of the multitudinous imperfect views of reality found in every case of finite experience. To us the world appears to be anything but perfect and thus, since according to absolutism it is perfect, each of us in our own ignorance is the incarnation of error. How then is the perfection of the Absolute reconciled with the actual existence of such cognitively defective creatures as we are? As James puts the problem:

Suppose the entire universe to consist of one superb copy of a book, fit for the ideal reader. Is that universe improved or deteriorated by having myriad garbled and misprinted separate leaves and chapters also created, giving false impressions of the book to whoever looks at them?[12]

What James is suggesting then is that if the Absolute is perfect, and if the resultant world is perfect in its eyes, would not the perfection of that Absolute better be maintained if its creative fiat had never brought into being all of us creatures of distorted understanding? We could have instead remained nothing but a perfect scheme existing ideally in the timeless view of the Absolute. "The scheme *as such* was admirable; it could only lose by being translated into reality."[13]

Should the absolutist respond to this by saying that the multitudinous imperfect views of things are logically required by the nature of things, he is abandoning monism and resorting to pluralism. For to make the being of the Absolute depend on its constituents is to allow the latter to develop selfhoods on their own accounts, and this is to leave the fortress of the Absolute. "The absolute as such has *objects,* not constituents," says James.[14] By this he means that, in keeping with the theory of the Absolute, the finite experience we are discussing must be accounted for as derived from this Absolute, as its objects. The Absolute qua Absolute is his own integral experience of things, and cannot be thought of as dependent on any finite mode of experiencing the world.

So the theory of the Absolute seems unable to give a satisfactory answer to the problem of evil. James puts forth his own finite God theory as handling this difficulty adequately. The problem is solved if we

> allow the world to have existed from its origin in pluralistic form, as an aggregate or collection of higher and lower things and principles, rather than an absolute unitary fact. For then evil would not need to be essential; it might be, and may always have been, an independent portion that had no rational or absolute right to live with the rest, and which we might conceivably hope to see got rid of at last.[15]

If we do not insist on instating rationality at the very foundation of all reality as the monist does, if we will allow something to escape ultimate inclusion, then the responsibility for evil in the universe can be divorced from the forces of goodness. And we need not then slip into the irrational position of showing how that goodness requires evil as the very condition of its goodness. James' finite theism escapes this latter difficulty.

The criticism of the Absolute in relation to the existence of evil appears to be quite different from the previous difficulties. Those points of criticism found the Absolute at fault because it prevented the fulfillment of certain human needs. The problem of evil, on the contrary, presents a rational incompatibility between certain objective facts and the nature of the Absolute. This seems like a purely speculative difficulty unrelated to human needs. But this is really not the case. The practical implications of this problem were never far from James' mind. In *A Pluralistic Universe,* after raising the theoretical difficulty discussed above, James goes on to add:

> In any pluralistic metaphysic, the problems that evil presents are practical, not speculative. Not why evil should exist at all, but how we can lessen the actual amount of it, is the sole question we need there consider.[16]

And in *The Varieties,* James immediately moves from the incompatibility of evil and the Absolute to the healthy-minded outlook that sees evil as something to be overcome. So even the problem of evil is related to the moral stimulant reason for James' finite God theory. Evil as something we must combat, rather than resign ourselves to, serves as a stimulating force for the healthy-minded. It becomes, in James' own words, a practical problem rather than a speculative one, and calls for the unleashing of our moral energies. Overall, it is accurate to say that, just as James affirmed the existence of God as a support for moral energies, likewise it is the dominating consideration in his reflections on the nature of God.

CRITICISM OF TRADITIONAL THEISM

James' criticism of traditional theism is much less extensive than his criticism of absolute idealism. This is accounted for by the fact that, philosophically speaking, absolute idealism had superseded traditional theism during this period. At Harvard, where James taught, Josiah Royce brilliantly represented the tradition of absolutism. He and James were close friends and philosophical foes for a quarter of a century. So it was absolute idealism that posed the most immediate target and called for the most sustained attack. Yet the older theism did not escape scrutiny altogether.

James praised traditional theism, as he had absolute idealism, for giving man a certain intimacy with the universe. With God as creator of the world, physical nature originates in a spiritual source that gives it a kinship with man. But there the praise ends. For theologians have been so insistent on maintaining a distance between God and creation that man becomes an outsider to this God. James compacts his criticism on this point into a single paragraph.

> The theistic conception, picturing God and his creation as entities distinct from each other, still leaves the human subject outside of the deepest reality in the universe. God is from eternity complete, it says, and sufficient unto himself; he throws off the world by a free act and as an extraneous substance, and he throws off man as a third substance, extraneous to both the world and himself. Between them, God says "one," the world says "two," and man says "three," —that is the orthodox theistic view. And orthodox theism has been so jealous of God's glory that it has taken pains to exaggerate everything in the notion of him that could make for isolation and separateness. Page upon page in scholastic books go to prove that God is in no sense implicated by his creative act, or involved in his creation. That his relation to the creatures he has made should make any difference to him, carry any consequence, or qualify his being, is repudiated as a pantheistic slur upon his self-sufficingness.[17]

This criticism is twofold. First, God, man, and the world are all distinct substances rather than being one, as in pantheistic theories. As we saw, James praises absolute idealism for making the human subject an integral part of the Deity. Why he finds this desirable will be discussed later. Second, in addition to our not being internal parts of God in traditional theism, there is an even more radical separation. God is totally removed from man, unaffected by him, and completely self-sufficient. He enters into no relationship with His creatures. He is utterly transcendent. The problem then becomes one of understanding how we can be meaningfully related to such a God who remains unaffected by our concerns and efforts.

Lest one wonder whether James is representing truly the traditional notion of God, it should be added that this same God is also understood as one who loves us, who providentially cares for us, and forever sustains us in our existence.[18] But these qualities are ones that theologians have interpreted in the context of God's transcendence. Thus, God's love for man must be understood in a fashion compatible with His being unaffected by us. So James' characterization of the traditional God is not wrong, though it appears unduly harsh when taken in isolation from the more tender side of that view.

As in the case of absolute idealism, James sees the lack of intimacy in traditional theism as diminishing man's place in the universe and shortcircuiting his moral energies. Man, in this view, does not have a creative place in the universe. While such creativity was made impossible in absolute idealism because of the "eternal completeness" inherent in God's timelessness, in traditional theism the same occurs because God, in His externality, is unaffected by us and stands as our eternal lawgiver.

> His actions can affect us, but he can never be affected by our reaction. Our relation, in short, is not strictly a social relation.
>
>   . . . .
>
> Man being an outsider and a mere subject of God, not His

intimate partner, a character of externality invades the field. God is not heart of our heart and reason of our reason, but our magistrate, rather; and mechanically to obey His commands, however strange they may be, remains our only moral duty.[19]

In talking about the strenuous mood we saw that it demands that man both be in a position to help decide what shall be, and that its realization depends on him, at least in part. Traditional theism, with God as lawgiver, deprives us of the first characteristic and absolute idealism with its timeless determinism deprives us of the second. James' finite God theory stands as a remedy to both.

It might be worthwhile to pause here over one point. Like many contemporary theists influenced by the spirit of our own age, James demands for man a more creative place in the world than the older theism allows. That view saw man as free, but the freedom allowed was a freedom to conform to God-given laws and structures of existence. It was not a freedom to create, to build a humanly satisfying world with man as at least partial architect. But with the advent of such factors as the theory of evolution and man's technological control over the world, the mentality of conformity has receded. The theory of evolution has taught us to look at the world in developmental terms, and our technological ingenuity has made the world we live in largely a product of our own doing. Human life itself, man's lived existence, is often thought of in terms of becoming. Not God-given commandments but the growth of the human person has come to be the focus of morality for many Christians.

In light of this newly dawning perspective and with great prescience regarding an outlook that would come to have a deep hold on the twentieth century, James affirmed a theistic view that would allow man a creative role in the universe. The open universe, almost synonymous with James' philosophy, briefly expresses this viewpoint. No longer could a view gain general acceptance which did not respect man's new understanding of himself and his relationship to the world. James thought of this creativity being exercised on our everyday world. In this activity we are partners with God, He being *primus inter pares*.[20] We are affected by Him and He by us in our common project of working to determine and secure the values that will shape our world. James did not think of our relationship with God as one whose primary purpose was the attainment of bliss in the next life. He certainly did not reject this possibility, but his concern was with securing for man a meaningful existence in this life. The creativity spoken of was an essential ingredient in this existence.

James does not pursue his criticism of traditional theism beyond the points mentioned. He adverts in places to problems this conception of God has with the existence of evil and with the timelessness of the Deity, but these are problems he discusses basically in relation to the Absolute. As was noted above, absolutism was the reigning conception and James felt it most imperative to contend with it. With this criticism of other positions in mind, let us look more closely at James' own conception of God, and discuss some of its more controversial aspects.

JAMES' CONCEPTION OF GOD

His conception of God is quite simple. Since it is not rooted in any metaphysical analysis of reality, it is not developed out of conclusions reached on the basis of such an analysis. In traditional theism, for example, God's timelessness, simplicity, and omniscience follow from the fact that God, as the terminus of metaphysical proofs for his existence, is understood as a self-subsistent act of existence. James' God, on the contrary, is simply constituted to assure the preservation of certain human values. The basic features of this God have already been indicated in the criticism of the theistic conceptions that James opposes.

God, as we saw, is finite in James' view. His finitude consists in the fact that, like us, He finds himself in an environment not totally of His own making. He is not an all-inclusive being and thus exists within the march of time and events. Some portion of reality escapes His dominion and is confronted as an obstacle with which He must contend. The extent and nature of this reality is a matter to which James gives little attention. What is essential is that God not exist in the all-form, not be totally inclusive of all that is. For if He does, He exists on a plane essentially different from man. He becomes timeless and totally responsible for the character of the world, and we are left with the irrationalities that follow. Thus God is finite in power and knowledge, and like us is a temporal being. "Having an environment, being in time, and working out a history like ourselves, he escapes from the foreignness from all that is human. . . ."[21] This conception is not internally incoherent since beings of this sort already exist— as in the case of man. God is like us in His essential characteristics, though obviously He is a greater, more inclusive being.

James' God is also immanent in His creation. James speaks of his own view as falling within "the pantheistic field of vision," with "God as the indwelling divine rather than the external creator."[22] We are internal parts of Him, "part and parcel of that deep reality," as he says.[23] His rejection of traditional theism was due to its dualism between God and His creation. He was attracted by the intimacy between God and man realized in absolute idealism. But this making one substance of the Divine and the human caused James difficulty. That difficulty lay in the question of how, if we are substantially fused with the Divine, we are at the same time our own individual selves. James certainly could not tolerate a conception wherein persons would be swallowed up into a greater whole that could cause them to lose their identity as distinct selves. That would run counter to the entire spirit of his philosophy, which is so intent on optimizing the value of the human. How then can we be both distinct selves and one with the divine?

In his later life James came to hold a doctrine called the "compounding of consciousness."[24] From Gustave Fechner, a nineteenth-century German philosopher of no great renown, James' awareness was aroused to the possibility that "the more inclusive forms of consciousness are in part *constituted* by the more limited forms."[25] Yet this more inclusive consciousness is not the mere sum of the more limited forms, just as our mind "is not the bare sum of our sights plus our sounds plus our pains, but in adding these terms together also finds relations among them and weaves them into schemes and forms and objects of which no one sense in its separate estate knows anything. . . ."[26] This inclusive form of consciousness still does not result in a loss of identity of the lesser states of consciousness, for "states of consciousness, so called, can separate and combine themselves freely, and keep their identity unchanged while forming parts of simultaneous fields of experience of wider scope."[27] What does this mean?

According to the commonsense point of view it would seem that a certain set of facts might be known by many minds, some of wider scope or more inclusive than others, and that each of these knowing processes would simply be itself and not the sum of less inclusive consciousnesses. For it to be itself and simultaneously be the less inclusive forms of consciousness, which latter all along maintained their identity, would seem to be a logical impossibility. James recognized this. Yet he took a position defying this logical impossibility, giving up the logic of identity "fairly, squarely, and irrevocably."[28]

Without claiming to do justice to his view here, this much

should be said. James felt that reality was richer than could be grasped conceptually. Lest our view of reality become impoverished, we must not feel constrained to respect the logic of concepts in formulating that view. Under the influence of Bergson's critique of intellectualism James came to accept a position that seemed contradictory when viewed in conventional terms. That view was that "mental facts do function both singly and together, at once, and we finite minds may simultaneously be co-conscious with one another in a superhuman intelligence."[29] We are individuals, yet submerged in the very life of God who is literally our life and more. We are constituent parts of God, and yet, simultaneously, our individual selves. This theory of the compounding of consciousness, then, underlies James' attempt to maintain a real plurality of selves in the face of their substantial identity with God.

A final point about the nature of God concerns the monotheism/polytheism issue. James did not take a firm stand on this point, but he did leave his theism open to a polytheistic interpretation. The superhuman level of consciousness, constituted out of the compounding of lesser consciousnesses, may involve a number of functionally distinct selves.[30] There may be a plurality, and possibly a hierarchy, of superhuman consciousnesses. James did not think that the data of religious experience testified unequivocally to the existence of a single God. Religious needs are adequately met if the power to which they appeal is large enough to take care of them.[31] Polytheism was hardly a possibility that James stressed, but within the confines of a theism built on the basis that his was, he found no absolute barriers to its acceptance.

While his position on the nature of God is far from the orthodox Christian notion, for the most part it is readily intelligible. This is not to say that it is true; it is not to say that it is without its own difficulties. But it does in a simple and straightforward way solve the difficulties it sets out to solve. A finite God lays to rest the problem of evil and does the same for theistic determinism. The one aspect of James' theory which is not so simple is its pantheistic element, making God and man one yet retaining the individuality of each. What important interests were served by introducing this complication into an otherwise simple theory?

The answer to this question seems to lie in the value of this conception for providing a framework for the divine/human relationship. In *The Varieties of Religious Experience* James speaks of the religious person as "continuous with a wider self through which saving experiences come. . . ."[32] A central theme in this book is the effect on the lives of human beings of living in the presence of the Divine. In the postscript to this work James contrasts what he calls "refined supernaturalism" with "piecemeal supernaturalism."[33] Refined supernaturalism accepts God but declares Him to be the inhabitant of a realm separate from that of His creatures. He does not intrude on that sector of existence. Science has a free reign to explain everything in its own terms because God is absent from the temporal order. While James granted that this view was in the ascendancy, he firmly rejected it in favor of piecemeal supernaturalism. The latter admits of the here-and-now workings of God in people's lives. This is not to be explained simply in psychological terms but must allow for the actual entrance of God into a person's life. What James' immanent theism does is to provide a way for understanding the workings of the Divine in human lives. If we are internal parts of God, forming the same field of consciousness though in different degrees, we have a ready framework for explaining the efficacy of the Divine in the human realm. There is no problem of understanding how a transcendent Deity, existing in an entirely different realm from ours enters our lives. The only barrier to the Divine affecting the human is the psychological one wherein the person bars himself from the wider life through self-imposed limitations. Erase this barrier and the Divine life can pour into the human realm, transforming it in just those ways described in *The Varieties of Religious Experience.*

Mysticism, to take an important instance of religious experience for which James had much respect, is easily explained if man is part and parcel of the Deity. Our conscious lives are limited forms of awareness within a larger conscious whole. For persons capable of overcoming these limitations, participation in a different form of consciousness is realized. We are already one with the larger consciousness and so any problem of union with a deeper reality melts away. It is truly the Divine encountered in mysticism. Thus, the immanence of God affords a way of explaining this phenomenon as something more than an interesting psychic occurrence.

But providing a framework for explaining how the Divine affects the human is only part of the story in James' philosophy. Of equal importance is how the human affects the Divine. We saw that James rejected the God of traditional theism because our relationship to Him was one of subservience to an independent lawgiver. James' vision is just the opposite. Man in the full and most meaningful exercise of his moral powers is a creative force in the universe. We and God are partners in deciding what shall be, and in bringing it about. Our actions then must be such as to be able to affect that God, just as He affects us in other contexts. Barriers to such communication again are broken down if we exist within that deeper reality that is touched by our actions. Since God's being includes our own, whatever we do necessarily affects Him. So James' pantheism serves an important purpose in providing a means for explaining this most vital aspect of his theism.

SOME CRITICAL CONSIDERATIONS

A few further points remain to be discussed about James' finite God theory. The deepest reason underlying this theory, as we saw, is its effort to secure a morally stimulating place for man in the universe. Is this value really incompatible with the forms of theism James rejects? Certainly the proponents of these theories interpret their positions as respecting important human values, such as man's freedom. The question then is, why didn't James give these theories a more extensive hearing than he did?

The answer, I believe, is twofold. First of all, he does have a more radical view of man's place in the universe than could be accommodated within these older forms of theism. Even the strongest proponents of those theories would find it difficult to incorporate the openness of James' universe into their own theistic framework. They might argue successfully for the inclusion of human freedom, but the creativity that James assigned to man lies beyond their scope.

The second reason why James did not give a more extensive hearing to these other theories is simply that he was not really interested in working out such an accommodation, even if it were possible. He thought that both absolute idealism and traditional theism, in the form in which he criticized them, were products of the philosopher's workshop. These "religious" conceptions had been developed "out of the resources of logical reason alone, or of logical reason drawing rigorous inferences from nonsubjective facts."[34] As such, they suffer from the thinness of all purely rational constructions. They are not rooted in experience, and they are not responsive to religious needs and experiences. We have already looked at James' criticism of this philosophical approach to religion in his dismissal of the arguments for God's existence. Here again the same issue is at stake. Given his objection to the basis on which these positions are established, he finds no need to interpret the values he finds important to accord with these older theories. A more straightforward approach is simply to formulate a conception of God in such a manner as to best preserve those values. This James did.

To say this is to touch on a central theme of James' theism, which is affirmed in both *Pragmatism* and *A Pluralistic Universe*. In those works he expresses the hope of convincing his readers that theism and empiricism can join hands in a happy union. Rationalism and theism have been partners over the ages but such intellectual support counts little for theism in an empirical age. James himself felt that rationalism was too far out of touch with reality to build a convincing case for theism. A favorite illustration of this he found in Leibnitz's solution to the problem of evil and his justification for eternal damnation. Quoting Leibnitz to the effect that it is the divine perfection along with the "principle of fitness" which necessitates all this suffering, he concludes that "Leibnitz's feeble grasp of reality is too obvious to need comment. . . ."[35] This feebleness results from allowing reason to run off on its own in the construction of religious concepts. It carries within itself a certain logical momentum, and inevitably ends up in conceptions that are far removed from what is demanded by man's experience. The philosopher at that point is obliged to reinterpret our ordinary experience and the ordinary meaning of words in an effort to reconcile them with the character and implications of the intellectual monster that has been created. Evil must be justified through the philosopher doing certain intellectual gymnastics to make the hideous accord with the perfection of the whole. The same gymnastics are necessary regarding the matter of giving meaning to our moral life, when that meaning appears to conflict with the implications of our intellectual constructs. Since James felt it was wrongheaded to intellectually construct religious objects in this way, he had little sympathy for the reinterpretations that followed.

His own approach was more empirical—to determine the nature of God so as to make it accord directly with the needs of our moral and religious experience. This is not to say that intellectual considerations have no part to play here. They do, but their role lies in such matters as determining what our moral needs really are, and in making sure that our religious concepts are not in conflict with other truths we hold. James speaks of the mind's function in relation to religion as "moderator amid the clash of hypotheses, and mediator among the criticisms of one man's constructions by another."[36] He adds further, regarding our "definition" of God:

> Philosophy can by comparison eliminate the local and accidental from these definitions. Both from dogma and from worship she can remove historic incrustations. By confronting the spontaneous religious constructions with the results of natural science, philosophy can also eliminate doctrines that are now known to be scientifically absurd or incongruous.[37]

So the intellect has a continuing role to play in our formulating a viable conception of God, but it is not the role of determining, on its own, what the nature of that God is.

The objection to this approach coming from rationalist quarters is that once we allow our conception of God to be determined by anything but reason working out of its own resources, or through reflection on objective facts, that conception becomes relative. For though we may work to purify it from historical encumbrances and local variations, we always do so from our present perspective, which is itself subject to change. And, further, to bring this conception of God into line with present scientific knowledge leaves it vulnerable to continuing change as new scientific plateaus are reached.

James does not deny that this is so, but he feels that this situation, for better or for worse, is unavoidable. What, he asks, is the alternative? Can we really cut our conception of the Deity out of purely rational cloth, objectively determining once and for all what his nature and attributes are? Can we accept forever in some unaltered form the nature of God as it was revealed to us in the scriptures? James' answer to both these questions is a firm no. To do that can too easily result in a conception of God that doesn't respect our needs, or that conflicts with other truths we hold. Such a God cannot really be believed in. This is shown if we look historically at the issue. We see that, in fact, people's conception of God has changed with changes in the overall mental climate.

> Nothing is more striking than the secular alteration that goes on in the moral and religious tone of men, as their insight into nature and their social arrangements progressively develop. After an interval of a few generations the mental climate proves unfavorable to notions of the deity which at an earlier date were perfectly satisfactory; the older gods have fallen below the common secular level, and can no longer be believed in.[38]

No God could be believed in by us today who required bleeding sacrifices, nor could we accept the Puritan God of Jonathan Edwards who arbitrarily dealt out salvation or damnation to select individuals. The mental climate is not right for such gods. They do not measure up to the common secular level that we impose even on ourselves.

What James is affirming is that there is no way we can jump out of our cultural skins to gain a time-transcending view of God. Our understandings of ourselves, the world we live in, and the nature of our relationships with each other, are the determining factors in what we can believe about God. As we discover more about the environmental causes of crime in our culture, the God of retributive justice grows less credible. As love becomes the therapy that heals all, a God who specializes in justice no longer satisfies us. As the workings of the physical world come to be understood as following scientific laws of nature, the God of miracles is laid to rest. The simple point is that our conception of God is tied to the mental climate that characterizes our culture. God supports our values and reinforces our ideals, and if He does not, He is altered or abandoned.

The nonrelativist in theological matters could counter James' position by pointing out that changes in our conception of God are not as radical as they might at first appear to be. Thus, while different attributes of God, such as love, justice, and mercy, may be stressed at different times in history, yet our conception of God's basic nature remains unchanged. And even if we thought of Him at one time as regularly dispensing miracles, and now do not, that too is an inessential part of our concept of God. Through it all, the basic nature of God as formulated with theological precision has really remained unchallenged.

No doubt there is much validity in this response to James' position. Any given age, sensitive to particular characteristics of ourselves and our world, might emphasize one aspect of God to the neglect of another. A new age may have a different emphasis, but both would agree on the basic nature of the Deity. However, this is not the whole story. There is impressive support among contemporary theologians for a more radical relativism in our thinking about God. Their approach tends to be more in line with that of James. They are reinterpreting the traditional doctrine of God in a way that, by any standards, bears on God's basic nature. And this is being done because our present mental climate is, in their judgment, incompatible with the traditional understanding of God. As Christian theologians they profess a fidelity to the scripture in their speculations, but these speculations nonetheless have the effect of a radical theological reformulation of our present conception of God.

Among Protestant theologians, Paul Tillich is most notable in this regard. He contends that theologians must be responsive to the contemporary situation rather than adhering to a too literal understanding of the scriptures. The contemporary situation he refers to is not the fluctuating mood of individuals or the general populace, but "the interpretations of human life and existence given by nontheological disciplines," such as science and philosophy.[39] Care must be taken not to reduce the Christian message to a simple reinforcement of the idols of a new age, but this danger must not prevent us from making God intelligible in the language of the present day. Out of this background arises Tillich's reinterpretation of God as "Being Itself." God is not to be understood as an objective entity, a supreme Being whom we face as other than ourselves. He cannot even be said to exist, since this assertion would be an infringement on His radical transcendence. It goes without saying that the pronouns *He* and *Him* used in reference to God in the previous sentence are also purely symbolic. Tillich's theology then goes beyond a change of emphasis in our thinking about God to a different way of understanding the Divine altogether, and this is done under the pressure of changes in the mental climate.

The same situation is found in Catholic circles. Gregory Baum is a clear instance. In his book *Man Becoming* he undertakes a reinterpretation of God that also does away with God understood as man's "over-against."[40] According to Baum, God is redemptively present to human life, and every sentence about Him must be able to be translated into a statement about our existence. There is no standpoint from which God can be viewed as an "other" facing man. This new doctrine of God has become necessary because man no longer understands His existence as he did when the classical view of God was formulated. As the title indicates, man is no static entity but is in a process of becoming, of creating himself, and God must be understood as an integral part of this process of creation. Baum singles out four areas in which the older theism clashes with man's new self-understanding. The first area concerns the power of prayer; the second is the assignment of a secondary importance to man's secular existence; the third is the viewing of life as obedience to a divine lawgiver; and the fourth is accepting the idea of the whole of history as having been providentially planned from the beginning by a supreme being.

Given this changed understanding of ourselves and of our relationship to the world we live in, a change in our conception of God is called for. The older theism cannot be stretched to accommodate certain important values that have become integral to our present existence. The result is a basic, not a peripheral, change in our thinking about God.

In the cases of both Tillich and Baum two things are clear. They do reinterpret our understanding of God in a radical way, and this is done under the pressure of man's changing understanding of himself and his world. Thus, the contention that the changes in our notion of God in different ages are no more than matters of emphasis is hardly the truth. Nor can it be said that Baum and Tillich are unique in respect to their radical dealings with the traditional notion of God. John MacQuarrie, certainly one of the most knowledgeable theologians writing today, goes so far as to say that just as modern theology has abandoned the God of mythology, it has likewise "grown doubtful about the God of supernaturalistic theism."[41] This departure from the supernatural certainly represents a radical change in our thinking about God.

James' basic approach to an understanding of God, then, is not without parallel in contemporary theological circles. We saw that he rejected a rationalistic elaboration of God's nature in favor of one that was more tuned to man's needs and to the mental climate in which we find ourselves. This involves the recognition that what man believes cannot be considered in isolation from the wider cultural context in which those beliefs exist. We cannot believe what doesn't make sense when considered in relationship to the understanding of the world found in other facets of our culture. This means that our concept of God is subject to change.

Overall, James' approach to God will not satisfy those who demand a final and definitively formulated position of God's nature. But it does have the strong point of recognizing that, factually speaking, there is no sense in clinging to a doctrine of God that has been made incredible by other changes in our understanding of the world.

So much for James' conception of God. This conception ties in neatly in James' own philosophy with his doctrine of pragmatism. Pragmatism, as he views it, ultimately champions an open, developing universe, and this process includes God himself. The rest of James' religious philosophy also shows the influence of his pragmatism, sometimes in a general and sometimes in a specific way. We will conclude our study of this philosophy with a consideration of the influence of James' pragmatism upon it.

5.

Pragmatism and Religion

At the end of the last chapter it was stated that James' pragmatism is related to his religious philosophy in both a general and a specific way. At the general level it is found in his empirical approach to religious problems, combined with his continued sensitivity to the needs of the religious person and to the benefits derived from religious belief. In this sense pragmatism is a spirit that pervades all of James' religious considerations. In a more specific way, as a technical theory of meaning and truth, pragmatism is also an important factor in his religious philosophy. As a theory of meaning it provides the basis for James speaking intelligibly of God, and it enables him to discard those divine attributes which he considers cognitively vacuous. As a theory of truth it provides the sense in which James, consistent with his own approach to religious questions, can speak of various beliefs as being true or false. This theory of truth is also integrally involved in his conception of the universe as open to change. Each of these points will be worked out in detail in this chapter of our study.

GENERAL PRAGMATIC ORIENTATION

If we take pragmatism to mean an approach to philosophical problems that is centered on their implications for human life, their fruits or practical results, then James' entire religious philosophy is pervaded by a pragmatic spirit. Pragmatic here is taken as opposed to speculative. A speculative approach to philosophical problems discusses them in wholly intellectual terms. It focuses exclusively on their rational cogency and is oblivious to what is at stake for the human person in the different possible answers to the questions. Such at least is the speculative ideal, though James and many others would question whether we can sufficiently shed our built-in cultural prejudices so as to attain this objectivity. The various arguments for the existence of God would be good examples of this speculative effort, as would be the attempt by the philosopher to reconcile the evil in the world with the divine perfection. The discussion in each case is carried out on the intellectual merits of the issue, and these merits are determined by our insights, or lack thereof, into the reality we are attempting to understand. Though the philosopher may be personally concerned about the outcome of his speculations, this does not formally enter into his considerations. As a speculative thinker his pose is one of detachment from anything other than the inner logic that drives him to his conclusion.

That the speculative model does not fit James is obvious from everything that has gone before in our considerations. True, as a philosopher, he does rationally justify his stand on the issues he deals with. But the center of his concern on these questions is always with the values at stake for human life. Our very first consideration in raising the God question in James' philosophy was the importance of religious belief in the life of the believer. This was not just a convenient way of getting into his philosophy, but instead it reflects a priority in his own thinking. He would not be concerned with the question of God at all if it did not carry important consequences for our lives. These consequences, as we saw, were the support gained to sustain one in the strenuous mood and the refuge provided when one's moral energies are spent.

The general pragmatic spirit of James' religious philosophy is reflected at a still deeper level. Not only does he point out the values at stake in religious belief, but he also argues that the values realized through any belief provide the impetus for trying to justify that belief. Science grows out of needs we want satisfied, demands that we place on the universe to show itself intelligible in a certain fashion. James' teleological view of the human mind as a center of interests and desires underlies this entire outlook. It is an easy matter to see the pragmatic outlook inherent in this view. The mind is no *tabula rasa* passively reflecting the nature of the universe in which it finds itself. Instead, it operates with ends in view, with needs to be satisfied. It demands this or that intellectual character of the universe, or this or that moral and religious character. The mind, as teleologically oriented, serves human interests. Philosophy is not an end in itself but serves the larger interests of life, insofar as it works to satisfy particular needs that we have. The pragmatic, in contrast to the speculative, character of this aspect of James' philosophy is immediately obvious.

If we turn to James' "will to believe" theory, this too can be seen as having a practical orientation. The reason that James is interested in justifying belief in the absence of decisive intellectual evidence is the loss of benefits that would result were such beliefs forbidden. To live as if a certain belief were not true when the matter is uncertain is to deprive the believer of the stimulus that comes with such a belief, and to deprive the rest of the world of the fruits that might come from actions springing from that belief. Again, it is the beneficial consequences that James has in mind when he argues for the right to believe.

Finally, when it comes to a question of the nature of God, here again it is the life values at stake that determine the issue. The basic reason underlying James' conception of God as finite is that this notion best provides for a morally stimulating life for man. The nature of God is decided not through any logical necessities, but because of the consequences involved for human life. The pragmatic orientation of this procedure is plain enough. Overall, then, James' considerations manifest a pragmatic spirit that shows itself in the central place he gives to the human implications of his religious theses.

We will likewise find the stamp of pragmatism in his religious thought if we consider pragmatism in its narrower sense of a theory of meaning. In what follows it will be necessary to deviate briefly from a direct consideration of James' religious philosophy so as to explain his pragmatic theory of meaning. Having done that, its relation to his religious thought will be made clear.

PRAGMATISM AS A THEORY OF MEANING

James proposes his pragmatic theory of meaning as a way of settling metaphysical disputes. Some disputes it settles by showing them to be mere verbal disagreements. Others are clarified in terms of their real meanings. In either case this is done by tracing the practical consequences of different concepts or thoughts. If these consequences are the same in both cases, then there is no difference of meaning in the supposedly different concepts, and the dispute is rendered idle. If the consequences are different, then we have a true basis for distinguishing the meaning of one concept from another. The acceptability of this procedure depends, of course, upon accepting a criterion of meaning which identifies meaning with the practical consequences a concept involves. It is this criterion which must be spelled out more clearly.

James tells us that we can specify a thought's meaning as follows:

> Thus to develop a thought's meaning we need only determine what conduct it is fitted to produce; that conduct is for us its sole significance. And the tangible fact at the root of all our thought-distinctions, however subtle, is that there is no one of them so fine as to consist in anything but a possible difference of practice. To attain perfect clearness in our thoughts of an object, then, we need only consider what effects of a conceivably practical kind the object may involve—what sensations we are to expect from it, and what reactions we must prepare. Our conception of these effects, then, is for us the whole of our conception of the object, so far as that conception has positive significance at all.[1]

The first point to note about this statement is that it is based on the contention that thinking is integrally related to action. Thinking is a guide to conduct, and thus, what a thought is about, what it means, can be determined by the conduct it is fitted to produce. Were thinking a sheerly intramental affair, this would not be so. In that case, distinctions could be made between different concepts which entailed no difference of behavior. It is this that James is denying. Thought for him is practical in the sense of being directed toward producing beliefs which govern our action. All differences in thought are manifested in the different conduct they inspire. "There can be no difference which doesn't make a difference—no difference in abstract truth which does not express itself in a difference of concrete fact, and of conduct consequent upon the fact, imposed on somebody, somehow, somewhere, and somewhen."[2] If thought and conduct are thus integrally related we should be able to determine the meaning of any thought by the "conduct it is fitted to produce."

The application of this criterion of meaning seems simple enough in concrete cases. For these cases involve sensations, and different sensations call for differences in conduct. An apple involves a conglomerate of sense qualities obviously not found in a tree or in water, and thus our reactions to each of these different objects will be different. We eat apples but not trees; we burn trees but not water, and so forth. Thus, what we mean by apple, tree, and water is easily distinguished according to James' criterion. And the difference lies in those varying sensations along with the different conduct they elicit from us.

More abstract notions do not involve the same sensory component and thus must be defined exclusively in terms of the conduct they produce. The idea of God is one that James uses to show how his criterion of meaning will work in these cases. The difference between theism and materialism, he says, cannot be adequately defined in simply aesthetic terms. Such a purely aesthetic distinction is found when the theist prefers to think of the world as rooted in spirit rather than in gross matter. The aesthetically inclined materialist responds by insisting that matter need not be thought of as gross, but as infinitely subtle and refined. This dispute between spirit and matter, in whatever form the latter is conceived, James finds idle. To get at the real difference between theism and materialism we must move beyond the aesthetic level and ask: "What practical difference can it make *now* that the world should be run by matter or by spirit?"[3]

The first point that James notes in response to this question is that it makes no difference at all unless the world has a future. Were we at the last moment of time, with the world ready to burn up and all conscious life to be forever consumed, there would be no difference between theism and materialism. If the results in both cases, so far as man is concerned, are the same—nothingness—then theism and materialism mean the same thing for us. The point James is making through approaching the issue in this fashion is to show that real differences between ideas must be spelled out in terms of their consequences for us. Unlike most theories of meaning, James' theory has a future orientation. The important question is, How will the future differ and how should I act in light of it? It is the answer to this question that constitutes the basis for distinguishing the meaning of different ideas.

Seen in this perspective, the practical difference between theism and materialism lies in the ultimate destiny of our universe. Materialism, affirming as it does the mindless evolution of matter as the deepest principle of the universe, leaves the world subject to final decay, and with it the dissolution of all the fruits of human labor. Nothing will be left that man cherishes. Human life will have been an insignificant episode, played out in a minute corner of the cosmos, with no ultimate significance whatsoever. Recall here James likening the human race to skaters on a lake of slowly melting ice from which there is no escape. That is the meaning of materialism. Theism, on the other hand, is the promise of an enduring moral order and with it the deeper significance that goes with human action.

> Materialism means simply the denial that the moral order is eternal, and the cutting off of ultimate hopes; spiritualism means the affirmation of an eternal moral order and the letting loose of hope.[4]

Thus, the materialism/theism issue is pregnant with consequences for human life, and it is in these consequences that the meaning of different ideas consists.

Recall here, too, James' discussion of the difference between his own finite God theory and the Absolute. That difference, so far as James was concerned, lay in the consequences of each conception. Regarding the finite God, "the conduct it is fitted to produce" is the morally strenuous life wherein man works hard for the achievement of ideals whose realization depends on him. The Absolute, on the other hand, means that all is cared for from eternity and man is granted a "moral holiday." James thought of these conceptions in terms of the reaction they called for from us, and thus they plainly manifest his pragmatic notion of meaning.

James' pragmatism not only enables him to define clearly certain religious conceptions, but it also enables him to eliminate others as meaningless. We saw earlier that he argues against determining the character of the religious universe through constructing "religious objects out of the resources of logical reason alone, or of logical reason drawing rigorous inferences from non-subjective facts."[5] This process results in religious conceptions cut wholly out of intellectual cloth, and without any significance for man's conduct. The metaphysical attributes of God are clear illustrations of this. God's aseity, immateriality, and simplicity, for example, may be flawlessly deduced by the systematic theologian, but they are "destitute of all intelligible significance."[6] How are we affected by the simplicity of God? "Pray, what specific act can I perform in order to adapt myself better to God's simplicity?"[7] And so it is with God's other metaphysical attributes as well.

When it comes to God's moral attributes, or His other attributes related to our well-being, the situation is different. God's mercy, love and power do mean something to us. Being loving and merciful, He wills our good and is ready to forgive. Being powerful, He can secure the triumph of the good. These attributes make a difference to man and must be taken into account by us in our outlook and conduct. James has little use for the support these attributes receive through the ratiocinations of systematic theologians, since the important support for religion comes from the experiential, rather than the intellectual, domain. But the attributes themselves are important and meaningful according to the pragmatic criterion.

Such is the way James lays out his criterion of meaning and the way he applies it to the religious realm. The most controversial application of this theory of meaning—and one that has an important bearing on his religious philosophy—is its application to the notion of truth. His pragmatic definition of truth raised a furor at the time of its publication, most critics contending that it denied the very notion of truth. James, for his part, maintained that he only spelled out what truth really meant in concrete terms, and that his critics were simply worshipping an abstraction. Of greatest importance for his religious philosophy is the fact that this notion of truth nicely supported the open and developing universe inherent in his conception of God. Let us turn now to this topic. Again, to consider the relationship of James' pragmatic theory of truth to his religious philosophy, it will be necessary to deviate temporarily from a direct consideration of his religious thought. This is necessary in order to spell out his pragmatic notion of truth. Having done this we will then be able to see its relationship to his religious thought proper.

THE PRAGMATIC THEORY OF TRUTH

The pragmatic theory of truth is an outgrowth of the pragmatic criterion of meaning. What we mean by truth must be spelled out in terms of its consequences. James has no difficulty in agreeing with his critics that an idea is true if it corresponds with reality, if it agrees with that reality. The dispute arises over what is meant by *correspond* or *agree with*. Usually no further elucidation is forthcoming, as these terms are thought to express clearly enough what we mean by calling an idea true. But James wanted these terms defined pragmatically. What are the consequences of an idea being true, of its corresponding with reality? The answer is quite simple. That idea "works" in respect to the object it is about. If it is true that a river is frozen, then when I look at it on a windy day I will see no waves, and when I step on it I will not sink to the bottom. If it is true that Washington was our first president, then when I read accounts of the history of this country I will find statements to that effect, when I read chronological lists of our presidents I will find his name on the top, when I refer to this fact in conversation no dispute will arise. These are easy examples, but they illustrate James' point clearly. Truth is a property of an idea and it means its ability to work. It performs the function of "agreeably leading" us through our experience. The truth of an idea consists in just such consequences—its workableness.

Most philosophers who speak about truth would say that an idea works *because* it is true. Truth, as correspondence between an idea and reality, is antecedent to the fact that a true idea proves to be workable. James, in pragmatically defining truth, insists that truth is constituted by the workableness, or as he sometimes says, the usefulness of an idea. What we mean by truth is this ability to work, to lead us agreeably, to be useful. Of an idea "you can say either that 'it is useful because it is true' or that 'it is true because it is useful'."[8] The point is that when we talk about truth we are talking about a particular property of an idea, a function it performs. That is what is meant by truth.

This theory as to the nature of truth follows from James' view of the mind as an active, selective agency. In this view the mind tries out ideas, it experiments. It comes to reality out of its own interests and needs. If this is the case, the measure of its success will be in terms of how well its ideas work in relation to the needs from which they spring, how well they lead us through experience. If, on the other hand, the mind were viewed as a mere detached spectator of the world, as basically receptive of a given reality in its cognitive life, truth would be understood in terms of the mind mirroring that reality. Another way of putting this overall point is by saying that, for James, the mind is practical. Its function is to put us into a successful working relationship with the reality we confront, to deal with it according to our needs. The goal of thinking is success in dealing with reality, success here meaning that which satisfies whatever needs we experience. Truth, then, will naturally be defined in terms of that success.

The practical character of the mind associated with James' theory of truth should not be thought of in narrow, materialistic terms. The practical or workable nature of true ideas does not refer to their facility in helping us to make a dollar. Instead, ideas are true which help us in practice, that is, in working with the world we face in all its dimensions. Such an impractical idea as God's love can be practical in this sense of the word, and it can be held as a true idea under certain conditions (which will be spelled out shortly). Likewise, abstract ideas can be practical. We bundle together in our minds similar perceptions so that in each encounter with a particular instance of something we need not treat it as a wholly new thing. Were it otherwise, life would be stalled at every point. The workableness of theories, too, means something far different from cash value in the literal sense. What must be kept in mind for a true understanding of the practical character of true ideas is James' view of the mind as teleological. With need or want at the source of our entire mental life, every idea, even the most theoretical, can be practical in his sense of the word.

Another important misconception to which James' theory has been consistently subjected, is the contention that it enables a person to hold as true what really isn't true, just so it works. This objection parallels the objection to the will to believe, that it justifies one in believing what is known to be untrue. James' response to this charge against his notion of truth is that it does not take into account what is necessary for an idea or theory to work:

> We must find a theory that will *work;* and that means something extremely difficult; for our theory must mediate between all previous truths and certain new experiences. It must derange common sense and previous beliefs as little as

possible, and it must lead to some sensible terminus or other that can be verified exactly. To "work" means both these things; and the squeeze is so tight that there is little loose play for any hypothesis. Our theories are wedged and controlled as nothing else is.[9]

For an idea to work and thus be accepted as true, it must fit in with the data of our sense experience, with other truths that we hold, and with abstract logical and mathematical relationships that we accept. I cannot believe, if I want to, that the paper I am now looking at is not paper. This does not fit in with my sense experience. I cannot accept as true that the sum of the two five-dollar bills in my pocket will enable me to purchase a twenty-five-dollar item. This is not consistent with certain mathematical relationships over which I have no control. Nor can I, on the spur of the moment, decide to believe that a lifelong friend is not a friend at all. I may say so, but I can't hold it as true unless I have some good reason to do so. Why not? Because this new notion does not fit in with other entrenched ideas of mine. If, on the contrary, fresh data arise which lend support to my doubting this friendship, the old and new ideas will clash and they must work themselves out to some satisfactory solution. Thus, to work means to fit in with certain givens in our experience, and these exert control over what can or cannot be accepted as true. In cases where the truth of an idea is not determined by the data at hand James allows subjective preference to assert itself. But even here this preference can operate only within the limits imposed by the coercive data that confront us.

Despite the stringent truth requirements that a statement must pass, James readily allowed that truth, according to this theory, is relative. Every idea is subject to the challenge of new data and new theories that may emerge. Later generations may repair or refute any of our ideas. Newtonian science was true in its day since it adequately accounted for the then known facts of the physical world. The work of Albert Einstein has shown its incapacity to incorporate newly discovered data. So its day of truth has passed, or if we would still like to call it true today, this truth will hold only for a certain level of observation about the world. In either case its truth is relative.

Though this assertion of the relativity of truth sounds offensive, a shortcoming in man's capacity to understand the world, James did not take it as such. He enjoyed breathing the freer air of an unsettled universe. Those who spoke of truth in an absolute sense were simply refusing to recognize that a developing world and new discoveries made today's truths subject to revision. We could, of course, through definition, make truth nonrelative by declaring it to be the agreement of an idea with reality, absolutely speaking. But these are just words without content so far as our form of experience is concerned. Perhaps a knower of a different and more godlike sort is capable of that sort of knowledge, but not us. Truth for us, concretely speaking, can only be the agreement of our ideas with the world which we experience. To speak of it differently is to take it out of the human domain.

Immediately following James' chapter on truth in *Pragmatism* is a chapter that further draws out the radically open-ended character of his universe. Entitled "Pragmatism and Humanism," it consists of an examination of the subjective factor, or human input, in our knowing of the world. Reality cannot be spoken of in any absolute sense. The reality we know is always a product of an objective factor which we confront in our experience plus a contribution from the side of the subject. This contribution varies with the interest and needs of the knower. Thus, reality, in the only form in which it enters our life and is meaningful to us, is no given or absolute, but a variable and fluctuating affair. The rationalist opponent of pragmatism, by way of contrast, is the proponent of a static reality. For him reality is something that stands ready-made, and to take account of what is simply given is our basic duty as knowers.

In this chapter James refers to the German philosopher Rudolf Hermann Lotze as having made the deep suggestion that the relation between reality and our minds may be just the opposite of what we naively assume it to be. We quite naturally think of reality as being given, with our duty as knowers being simply to describe it. But it may be that our own descriptions are important additions to reality, reality itself being there to serve as a stimulus for our minds to cast it into one shape or another. In the latter case reality is really malleable and receives its definitive touches from our hand. This, says James, is the pragmatist's conception and it is in radical opposition to that of rationalism.

> The essential contrast is that *for rationalism reality is ready-made and complete from all eternity, while for pragmatism it is still in the making, and awaits part of its complexion from the future.* On the one side the universe is absolutely secure, on the other it is still pursuing its adventures.[10]

James goes on to add that the alternative between pragmatism and rationalism thus turns out to be more than a difference in theories of knowledge. It is a difference which concerns the very structure of the universe itself. On the one hand we have a universe in process, developing in all its dimensions, including even the supernatural. On the other hand, the universe is a finished reality.

After this long detour, it is time to consider how this theory of truth, and its related humanistic conception of the universe, fit into James' religious philosophy. The answer is not far to seek. Essentially, it provides theoretical support for his form of theism. The radically open universe of the pragmatist is the same universe we met in discussing James' finite God theory. There it was his insistence that man have an efficacious role in helping shape the universe that necessitated God being finite and the universe being in process. Here it is his pragmatic criterion of meaning, eventuating in his theory of truth, that underlies this conception of the universe. Truth is a property of our ideas, bearing on the question of their relationship to the reality they are about. So long as truth is understood in relative and changing terms, the same must be the case for the reality it is about. Were James to understand truth as a conformity of the mind to reality, and also hold that truth of an absolute sort were attainable, we would, to be consistent, have to hold that an unchanging reality existed of which the mind could be aware. But while he accepts the notion of truth as the correspondence of the mind to reality, the truth attainable by human beings is a fluctuating one, and therefore it makes no sense to speak of the reality it is about as being anything but changing. If truth is mutable and is at the same time cognizant of reality, then reality itself is mutable. We can, of course, posit a different and immutable reality in some realm unattainable by man, but this is simply an ideal that has nothing to do with the actual truth and reality as it is present in man's life. And this latter is all that we can speak meaningfully about.

Thus, James' theory of truth supports his view of reality as radically open to change. As such, it fits nicely into his theistic universe. For that universe in all its dimensions, God included, is in process. God Himself is finite; He is subject to being influenced by us; and with mankind He is working toward the creation of a world of maximum value. Recall, too, the importance God has for human life. This fits into the open universe of pragmatism, for it is essentially in providing support for our efforts in shaping an open-ended world that God is needed. James concludes that "pragmatism can be called religious, if you allow that religion can be pluralistic or merely melioristic in type" in contrast to the monism that situates us in an essentially static world.[11]

It is also necessary to understand James' notion of truth in order to make sense of various assertions in his writings on religion. Take the following as an example:

> Her only test of probable truth is what works best in the way of leading us, what fits every part of life best and combines with the collectivity of experience's demands, nothing being omitted. If theological ideas should do this, if the notion of God, in particular, should prove to do it, how could pragmatism possibly deny God's existence? She could see no meaning in treating as "not true" a notion that was pragmatically so successful. What other kind of truth could there be for her, than all this agreement with concrete reality?[12]

This statement sounds as if James is asserting that we can say that "God exists" is a true assertion even when it is not or might not be. The reason it sounds this way is that, ordinarily, when one says that it is true that God exists, one means that, as a matter of absolute fact, there is some objective reality existing that we designate by the term God. If there is no such objective reality existing, then we cannot say that it is true that God exists. According to James' understanding of truth, however, to say that it is true that God exists means certain concrete happenings within human experience. It means that when I act on the idea of God's existence, it fits harmoniously into specific elements of my conscious life. It is supported, or at least not contradicted, by my sensible experience. It fits in with other truths I hold. And it satisfies certain demands I place on the world. Pragmatically speaking, this is what it means to say that some assertion is true.

The nonpragmatist maintains that when he says something is true, this refers to the bare fact that what is affirmed mentally also obtains factually. For the pragmatist this fact is a little too bare. Pragmatically speaking it means nothing. Still, when James lays out what he means by saying that it is true that God exists, he is not denying what the nonpragmatist asserts. He is only saying that, when someone says that X or Y is true, he can mean nothing but the concrete workings that the pragmatist spells out as constituting the truth of an idea.

Certainly this is a relative notion of truth. An idea's working in relation to certain other factors in our experience is always going to be relative to whatever other factors we happen to be aware of. The nonpragmatist asserts that truth is something that is absolute in the sense that, when an assertion is true, what it is true of exists in itself, as a definite reality. James contends that this is fine as an ideal, but concretely speaking, what does it mean? In our actual cognition of reality all we can realize is what the pragmatist spells out as the essence of truth. No more can be attained. So to speak of truth as something that is other than this is to speak of it in a fashion that is not humanly attainable. Truth in the only sense in which it is meaningful to us is truth as it is realized in our experience. Anything beyond this is meaningless.

Thus, to understand fully what James means by various assertions that find their way into his reflections on religion, it is important to understand his notion of truth. He can call true certain ideas which, by other standards or notions of truth, would not merit that title. Whether or not one agrees with him in these assertions depends on whether one agrees or disagrees with his pragmatic elucidation of the meaning of truth.

The net effect, religiously speaking, of these considerations about James' theory of truth is twofold. First, this theory supports his religious view of the universe as in a process of becoming. And, second, to understand what he means when he calls a religious assertion true, we need to understand his underlying notion of truth. We also saw earlier how James' pragmatic criterion of meaning was at work in his religious philosophy, and how in a more general sense this entire philosophy is pervaded by a pragmatic spirit.

6.

Some Final Comments

In these final comments I would like to offer a brief summary, interspersed with evaluative comments, of certain major aspects of James' religious thought. I will also note some respects in which he has been a forerunner of twentieth-century theological concerns. Before getting into the specifics of this, however, a brief preliminary comment regarding the evaluation of his philosophy is in order. In the Introduction to this study the point was made that James' reflections on religion were geared toward considerations which could help the individual in his existential dilemma of belief or unbelief. How to help the flesh-and-blood person experiencing difficulties as a believer was James' central interest. Consequently, any attempt to judge the merits of his religious philosophy must take this intention into account. He must not be criticized for not doing what he never intended to do. The remarks that follow will respect this intention inherent in his philosophy.

BELIEF IN GOD

It is not surprising that we find James giving the attention he does to the importance of God in our lives. This is in keeping with the general pragmatic orientation of his philosophy. But even leaving this pragmatism aside, this interest in the importance of religion is not unexpected. Once the reality of God becomes a question for an individual, or a culture, it is the needs that religious belief fulfills that take precedence. The loss of God, or the threat of that loss, is experienced in terms of how our lives are diminished without God. In our deeper moments we know that of ourselves we are subject to death, that ultimately our doings amount to nothing, and that very often we are powerless to carry out successfully our most cherished quests. Mankind is not made to accept this ultimate nothingness of his being or his efforts, and his refusal to do so impels him to cling to the idea of God no matter how severe the challenge to the integrity of that belief may be.

It is a great merit of James' philosophy that he remained sensitive to this religious dynamic of man at a time when it was not intellectually fashionable to do so. While other philosophers were clamoring to proclaim man's independence of God and his coming of age, James continued to affirm the deeper truth that without God man is subject to despair and nothingness. He was not so much concerned about the reality of God as a means for enabling man to overcome death, but he was very much concerned about God as a foundation of meaning and as a source of strength for us in the midst of our helplessness. As the foundation of meaning, God is an ally of man in his strenuous efforts, assuring him of the significance and lastingness of his achievements. Without that assurance, man, in his reflective moments, can easily fall prey to despairing about the value of his efforts, thus sapping his energies and diminishing the intensity and significance of his life. As a source of strength in his helplessness, belief in God enables man to cling to the worth of his existence despite the fact that he is confronted by failure in those things that matter most. In the "eyes of Him who really matters" we are still worthwhile, or in some more ultimate scheme our efforts are contributing to success. Such are the needs that God fulfills. James rightfully insisted on the reality of these needs and of their crucial importance for man in his deeper moments. If these are ineradicable human needs, bearing on those matters most dear to man, then without their fulfillment man's life loses its most needed support. Truly our lives are absurd if what we most need and want is that which we cannot possibly secure.

This insistence on man's religious needs is certainly not new with James. Augustine's well-known utterance, "Our hearts are restless till they rest in Thee," shows the same concern, and he was doing no more than affirming what many others felt and said. Yet this truth can easily be forgotten, and it is to the credit of James that he proclaimed it loudly in the face of equally contrary sentiments and concerns of others. In our own day, in the face of equally contrary sentiments, we find the same message being reiterated by a few thinkers. Paul Tillich and Langdon Gilkey are good examples of this among theologians. Karl Jaspers, the German existentialist, is a ready example from the ranks of the philosophers. Let me elaborate briefly on James' affinity with each of these thinkers.

Tillich, in *The Courage to Be,* analyzes the sources of the deep-seated anxieties that are intrinsic to the human condition. He sees man's life as threatened by various forms of "nonbeing" which give rise to different types of anxiety. He speaks of the "anxiety of fate and death," the "anxiety of emptiness and meaninglessness," and the "anxiety of guilt and condemnation."[1] Different ages are more prone toward one or the other of these anxiety types but, in any case, they must be dealt with at a spiritual level since they affect the human spirit as such. They are not medical problems, but arise out of the very conditions of human existence. Only through man's relation to the "unconditional" can they be dealt with adequately. Or, to phrase it differently, the ultimate in man's life must be such that it enables him to withstand this threat of nonbeing to his existence. It is not too difficult to see that these reflections fall into the same category as those of James when the latter probes the contingency of human existence and the other sources in man that give rise to religion. He too found that man without God is subject to meaninglessness and despair and that only in relation to a deeper power in the universe is the human quest for meaning and salvation satisfied.

Langdon Gilkey, in some interesting chapters in *Naming the Whirlwind: The Renewal of God-Language,* reflects on the adequacy of the secular model of existence that is seemingly in ascendancy today. This secular man is a completely this-worldly creature who interprets his life as the outcome of mindless forces which he must control as best he can in constructing, autonomously, his own world. Gilkey insists on the shallowness of this view and contends that we can live meaningfully only in a "context of ultimacy." He seeks

> to show that within ordinary secular experience, that deeper range, which we have called that of ultimacy and which religious language seeks to conceptualize, does appear; that in fact we are aware of it; that many of our interior feelings and anxieties are concerned with it; that our public or historical behavior is affected by it; and that we do talk about it all the time, whatever our explicit conceptualizations of experience may say or admit. If all this is so, then religious symbolism of this range of experience is shown to be both meaningful and necessary if life is to be human.[2]

Through a hundred probing pages Gilkey uncovers depths of existence that only religion can deal with adequately. The relation to James is again plain to see. The latter, less systematically but just as firmly, insisted on this religious dimension of human existence that must be confronted if man is to live his life most meaningfully. The context of ultimacy of which Gilkey speaks was likewise then an integral part of James' view of man.

To mention the name of Karl Jaspers in relation to James

is to bring up the latter's often discussed relation to existentialism and phenomenology. While there is an extensive literature on this topic, a full discussion of this relationship would take us too far afield.[3] For present purposes it is important only to note that Jaspers' "quest for transcendence," like James' affirmation of God, arises out of his reflections on the human condition. In previous ages it was man's sense of wonder about the world (Aristotle) or his effort to overcome scepticism (Descartes) that led him to philosophy. Today, it is the recognition of human finitude that is the moving force. The collapse of the Enlightenment ideal of creating an ever more perfect society has brought home to us, with an unusual poignancy, our very real limitations. While man has far greater control over the physical world today than ever before, and while there are many problems that we can deal with adequately on our own, still we are confronted by what Jaspers calls "ultimate situations."

> I must die, I must suffer, I must struggle, I am subject to chance, I involve myself inexorably in guilt. . . . In our day-to-day lives we often evade them, by closing our eyes and living as if they did not exist. We forget that we must die, forget our guilt, and forget that we are at the mercy of chance. We face only concrete situations and master them to our profit, we react to them by planning and acting in the world, under the impulsion of our practical interests. But to ultimate situations we react either by obfuscation or, if we really apprehend them, by despair and rebirth: we become ourselves by a change in our consciousness of being.[4]

If we are not to accept the ultimate futility of our state we must transcend these limits by orienting our life toward a deeper reality. The parallel with James is too obvious to need comment.

In each of these instances—in the thoughts of Tillich, Gilkey and Jaspers—we find in twentieth-century form the same sense of the inadequacy of man alone that was central to James' own experience. In fact, the question of the meaning of life has become more widespread in our time than it was previously. To speak of "the encounter with nothingness"[5] or the "experience of nothingness"[6] is to speak a language that seems to have become commonplace. Tillich, Gilkey and Jaspers all find this threat of meaninglessness intrinsic to the human condition and turn to a religious analysis of man to deal with it. In so doing they again sensitize us to the problem James dealt with in similar form. It is to their company that he belongs.

Let us turn now from this brief excursion into James' contemporary counterparts and recall how he handled the religious problem that he had raised. Given the recognition that man is basically a God-seeking creature, what is he to do, the *he* here referring to the contemporary reflective man who experiences his "God need," and who is simultaneously plagued by doubts about the reality of that which he seeks to believe in? James' final answer to this question is: believe. But for this to be even possible for the person who is experiencing doubts, such belief must be rendered credible. For James this credibility cannot be achieved through the construction of any metaphysically elaborated proofs for the existence of God. These might be effective if man were simply an intellect and nothing else, but such is not the case. Consequently, more concrete and persuasive considerations are in order. Again, we must remember that James' interest and intention are in helping people to concretely confront the problem of belief.

His first step in this direction was to examine the primary cause of religious doubt—science. If its challenge could be blunted the believer's main obstacle to belief would be overcome. And science surely is that obstacle. Its ordering of all phenomena in terms of natural causes has given us a world from which the supernatural is absent. In the words of Brand Blanshard, "The mental atmosphere created by modern science, with its preoccupation with natural processes, its penchant for the measurable and its insistence on empirical evidence, is an atmosphere in which beliefs tend to wither away. . . ."[7] In much the same vein Walter Stace, in his *Religion and the Modern Mind,* analyzes the demise of religious belief at the hands of science.[8] What need to invoke God as a presence in our world when all that happens can be explained in purely natural terms? Most certainly this form of explanation does not disprove the existence of God, but it presents us with a world which very conceivably may have arisen out of, and operate in accordance with, scientifically discoverable laws and nothing else. That may be all there is at work in the construction and operation of our world. This certainly is the possibility that haunted James' mind.

In response to this possibility, he attempted to show the partial character of science's account of reality. Like all constructions of the human mind, it is selective. It pays attention to a particular aspect of that which it studies and it constructs its explanations in accordance with the interests from which it springs. Thus, it need not be accepted as an all-encompassing explanation of reality. Science's much lauded objectivity occurs within the confines of its partial perspective, and it should not be mistaken for an exclusive, disinterested account of the real. This line of attack on scientism is one that has been further developed in this century, especially within the movement known as phenomenology,[9] and it is a sound plank within James' efforts to restore credibility to belief in God.

His reflections on religious experience were also meant to add weight to his case for belief in God. He never developed any argument from religious experience for the existence of God, but he did attempt to defuse objections to the veridicality of this type of experience. His argument against medical materialism and his support of mysticism were instances of this. But the primary thrust of his reflections on religious experience was to show the power and value of religious belief in the lives of its adherents. This comes out clearly in *The Varieties of Religious Experience*. Religious belief enables the person to cope with life's ills, and it is an inexhaustible source of energy and vitality. And this consideration brings us back to where we began—with the importance of religious belief.

This importance certainly is the focal point of James' defense of religious belief. He basically argues as follows. If there are no forbidding objections to belief in God, and if such belief fulfills deeply experienced human needs and adds positively to our lives, then we should not feel compelled to refrain from such belief. This is the real meaning of James' own assertion that he believes in God because he needs him. His "Will to Believe" is a defense of this position. What must be kept in mind in considering this thesis is that James is talking about belief in that toward which we are moved by the deepest inclinations of our existence and which fulfills our most fundamental needs. Without such beliefs our lives are radically diminished. Given this context, James can find no reason why we must put a stopper on our instincts and live as if these beliefs were not true.

Though this "will to believe" thesis has been subjected to much criticism, I do not find fault with it. What James is attempting to do is to chart a course for those who are strongly inclined toward religious belief, but who feel that belief threatened. What to do in that circumstance is his question. For the philosopher to insist that one must continue to analyze the God question and deal with it only in terms of objective proofs and disproofs is no answer. It does not resolve the concrete issue the person is facing. James, like most philosophers today, saw no possibility of such proofs being valid nor of their being persuasive even if they were forthcoming. So he encouraged belief as an answer to the human needs involved. Though this belief might not be free of doubts about its object, it could serve as a basis for action and give the hope that man's deepest needs were not without an affirmative answer.

The philosopher qua philosopher may have little respect for James' line of thought. He would prefer to deal with the God issue for its own sake, and he might even relish keeping it alive as a problem. There is nothing wrong with this. James himself would not encourage anyone to avoid the intellectual dimensions of the issue. But as we have seen, his primary interest was in helping the human being come to grips with the issue in such a fashion as to be able to deal with it practically. In this respect I believe he has made a worthwhile contribution.

THE NATURE OF GOD

The least satisfactory side of James' religious philosophy is his conception of God. He postulated a finite God so as to leave the universe open to man's input and creativity and also to explain the existence of evil in the world. And, as we saw, he thought of this God in pantheistic terms. He also left his conception of God open to a polytheistic interpretation, though he never attempted to work this out in any detail. What Perry says regarding James' view of God seems to be true. While "he was essentially a man of faith, . . . he was not interested in the elaboration and specific formulation even of his own personal beliefs."[10] He did know what values must be made compatible with the nature of God, and he did find other views of God clashing with those values. His own finite God theory was proposed as a means of handling this problem, but James was not really interested in formulating this theory in any precise fashion. He was not the patient, systematic theologian tying all the pieces together into a manifestly coherent conception.

Even at the general level that characterizes James' proposed finite God theory, one must wonder about its viability.

Does it really serve the needs he cherishes? To speak of God as an ally in the pursuit of our ideals is fine, but if that God or those gods is or are finite, then He or they might be as much subject to ultimate defeat by a wider cosmic challenge as we would be, were we left to face the challenge of our world unaided. Thus, a finite God might not solve the problem James wants solved but only raise it to a different level. It is unsatisfactory for James to say in response to this difficulty that God must be conceived of as sufficient to work effectively in the face of any challenge. Unless a relationship between God and the reality he faces is worked out which shows that this is indeed the case, we do not even know that it is possible. James never worked out such a relationship.

Along different lines, there are still other questions which his theory leaves unanswered. Even if a finite God fills the needs which he finds important, does that God fit with the Divine as encountered in the religious experience which James himself describes? Does not the mystical experience of which he speaks seem to testify to a boundless, infinite Being? Or, if we read the pages of Rudolph Otto's *Idea of the Holy*, can we reconcile the Divine encountered there with James' finite God? In short, even if a finite God would fit the experienced needs James speaks of, would that God also fit the religious experiences elaborated elsewhere?

While there are problems in James' conception of God, what is most interesting and fruitful about his theory are the reasons and principles governing it. He is convinced that our conception of God is a relative one which must be brought into line with our understanding of our world and our selves. A God has no chance of being believed in unless He respects the values we hold dear. Of major interest to James is a conception of God that will preserve a creative role for man in the universe. In this respect he is a forerunner of twentieth-century theology. Unlike Nietzsche, who thought that God must die for man to become fully alive, James tried to reconcile a God whom we deeply need with a more creative place for man in the world. His immanent and finite God was the answer.

Theological thinking in this century has continued to be sensitive to the demand for creativity on man's part, and it has found the God of classical theism difficult to reconcile with this creativity. Walter Stokes, in an article entitled "God for Today and Tomorrow," speaks of a widely felt "tension between the dignity intrinsic to man's creative freedom on the one hand, and, on the other, the threat to that dignity posed by a God who is wholly transcendent."[11] Robert Johann distinguishes between the "freedom to conform" and the "freedom to innovate," the former characterizing man's relationship to the transcendent God of traditional theism, the latter expressing the creative role demanded by a more contemporary vision of man's relation to the world.[12] Theists sensitive to this demand have tried to satisfy it through stressing the immanence of God in the world. This is true of theologians inspired by Alfred North Whitehead's view of the world as in process. It is also the case with other thinkers as diverse as Paul Tillich and Gregory Baum. This stress on immanence has taken the form of moving away from God conceived of as a supernatural being, as with Tillich and Baum, or toward a developing, responsive God, as is the case among the Whiteheadians. Let us take a closer look at each of these approaches.

Tillich, as we saw earlier,[13] speaks of God as "Being Itself" rather than as a being, even a supreme and perfect being. Since God does not exist as an entity apart from his creation, but as the "ground" and innermost reality of all that is, a new relationship between God, man and the world can be worked out. Speaking not only of Tillich, but also of a number of other major contemporary theologians, Paul Santmire comments:

> For them, God or the "ground of being" is always acknowledged *within the given historical and natural milieu of*

human experience. Their legacy, then, was their emphasis on the matrix of concrete experience as the locus of ultimate meaning. Ultimate meaning is to be found in, with, and under the whole field of human existence, not in some Wholly Other heavenly realm.[14]

While James never spoke of God as the ground of being, the above statement surely expresses his own theistic interests— that meaning be located in our present experience and that God be conceived of as a reality within that experience.

Whitehead and the theologians inspired by him represent another approach to theism that exhibits the same basic concerns that James had. A fundamental interest among these thinkers is to redo the older theism so as to bring God into a reciprocal relationship with the world. The Deity is so conceived as to include the world in His very being while yet transcending it, He being thought of as having both a primordial and a consequent nature. It is this consequent nature which is inclusive of the world in its historical process. God and this world exist in enduring interaction, each depending on the other for its completeness. Thus, "it is equally true to say that the world creates God as it is to say that God creates the world" since they exist in a state of "mutual immanence."[15] Obviously, this is quite a different approach to God from the one we find in Tillich. But in both cases there is a similar interest in working out a new relationship between God and the world, one that will place them in a state of interaction and thus allow for a more creative role for man in shaping his destiny. Relating this to James, it can be fairly said that a major concern that faces these theologians today is the same concern that James grappled with almost a century ago, and certain directions that he followed in his attempted solutions are the very avenues being explored today. Whatever we may think of his effort to deal with these issues, there can be little doubt that he helped articulate and bring to a head certain problems that have become prominent in twentieth-century religious philosophy.

If we look, then, both at James' effort to make a case for belief in God and at his reflections on the nature of God, we find a number of respects in which he was a forerunner of present-day theological concerns. More might be added to what has already been said. While we have seen a relationship to later developments in James' sensitivity to man's religious needs and in his insistence on a theism that allows for human creativity, at a more basic level another obvious affinity with the present situation should be noted. In the last two decades the question of the existence of God has come to be a central question in theology. Following the 1962 publication of Bishop John Robinson's *Honest To God,* a flood of like-minded literature on the God question was released. Robinson's book expressed the concern about the reality of God that was oppressing the Christian community itself. Even the believer was not immune from the secular challenge inherent in the wider culture. As we have seen, the same question was the focal point of James' religious thought. While he remained a believer he experienced in his own life the full power of the emerging secular world view. It would not be too much to say that James in his day lived through the challenge to the existence of God that has become widespread in recent years. Here again he becomes a forerunner of an important aspect of the twentieth-century experience.

In the area of method James also provided a direction for later thinkers. His *Varieties of Religious Experience* signaled a turn toward the examination of religious experience in the discussion of religion and its beliefs. A more careful consideration of the actual dynamics of that experience and what it testifies to has become commonplace in this century. Along with this turn toward experience has gone a de-emphasis on natural or rational theology, as was also the case with James.

All of this is in keeping with the general empirical orientation that prevails amongst philosophers of religion today and which was a hallmark of James' own thinking.

Another affinity which he shares with later religious thinkers is his concern with the problem of meaning. This problem has come to play a large part in theological discussions in the last fifty years. Challenged by such works as A. J. Ayer's *Language, Truth and Logic,* the theist has had to defend the meaningfulness of his discourse about God before even raising the question of its truth. According to Ayer and the logical positivists, for an assertion to be cognitively meaningful it must be verifiable, or at least falsifiable. Unless some observable state of affairs counts for or against the truth of an assertion, it literally means nothing. Despite the fact that the logical positivist's criterion of meaning, in its strict sense, finds few adherents today, still the sensitivity to the question of the cognitive meaningfulness of theological assertions remains prominent. It lives on through the more subtle views of Wittgenstein who, through his *Philosophical Investigations,* suggests that the question of meaning should be discussed in terms of the use of language, and that the many language games we engage in can be meaningful in different contexts. Thus, in one form or another, the question of meaning has continued to dominate much of contemporary philosophy. This, too, as we saw was part of James' concern. His pragmatic criterion of meaning was meant to call into question the meaningfulness of theological assertions that had been generated out of rationalistic considerations alone. While that criterion was not identical with those that followed it in this century, it again represents the same concern that has since come to have a much wider hearing.

It is not my intention in noting these affinities between James' religious thought and that of our own day to pass judgment on the actual extent of his influence on later thinkers. This is always difficult to estimate. But I do think that it shows him to be our contemporary in terms of the problems he dealt with and the form in which they presented themselves. As stated before, whatever the final judgment may be on James' religious philosophy, it can safely be said that at the end of the last century he helped articulate those concerns that theologians since then have felt compelled to deal with. Like every genius he felt the force of certain tendencies in our culture before they became part of the common consciousness. Certainly he will have had the last word on few of these issues, but he felt their impact very keenly, helped bring them to an articulated awareness, and provided provocative suggestions for their resolution. A reading of his works today can still help us toward the resolution of our own problems.

Notes

1. See Hans Linschoten, *On the Way Toward a Phenomenological Psychology,* edited by Amedo Georgi (Pittsburgh: Duquesne University Press, 1968); Bruce Wilshire, *William James and Phenomenology* (Bloomington: Indiana University Press, 1968); John Wild, *The Radical Empiricism of William James* (New York: Doubleday, 1969).
2. Williams James, *The Letters of William James,* edited by Henry James (Boston: Atlantic Monthly Press, 1920), vol. 2, p. 58.
3. William James, *Pragmatism* (New York: Meridian Books, 1955), p. 33.
4. Julius Seelye Bixler, *Religion in the Philosophy of William James* (Boston: Marshall Jones, 1926). A more recent work by Eugene Fontinell, though not specifically devoted to James' religious philosophy, does attempt to use the philosophical insights of pragmatism toward a present-day "reconstruction of religion": *Toward a Reconstruction of Religion* (New York: Doubleday, 1970).

5. See, for example, Langdon Gilkey, *Naming the Whirlwind: The Renewal of God Language* (Indianapolis: Bobbs Merrill, 1969), pp. 10–11; or John Macquarrie, *God and Secularity, New Directions in Theology Today,* vol. 3. (Philadelphia: Westminster Press, 1967), pp. 14–15.
6. Ralph Barton Perry, *The Thought and Character of William James* (Boston: Little, Brown, 1935), vol. 1, p. 323.
7. Ibid.
8. Edited by Ralph Barton Perry (New York: Longmans, Green, 1912).
9. See especially Gregory Baum, *Man Becoming* (New York: Seabury Press, 1970), p. 164. See also Gilkey, pp. 36–39, 56–57.
10. Baum, pp. 164–65. Gilkey, pp. 36–39, 58–59. Macquarrie, pp. 103–4. See also Walter Stokes, S. J., "God for Today and Tomorrow," *The New Scholasticism,* 43 (Summer, 1969), pp. 351–78.
11. Terence Penelhum, *Religion and Rationality* (New York: Random House, 1971), chaps. 16, 18, 21. Nelson Pike, *God and Timelessness* (London: Routledge and Kegan Paul, 1970), chap. 4. Fontinell, pp. 196–208.
12. Baum, chap. 6. John Macquarrie, *Thinking About God* (New York: Harper and Row, 1975), especially chap. 9 and "How We Can Think of God," as found in *Philosophy Today No. 2,* edited by Jerry Gill (London: Macmillan, 1969), chap. 7. Paul Tillich, *Systematic Theology* (3 vols.; Chicago: University of Chicago Press, 1967), vol. 1, pp. 235–89, and *The Courage to Be* (New Haven: Yale University Press, 1952), pp. 182–90.

CHAPTER 2

1. William James, *The Varieties of Religious Experience* (New York: New American Library, 1958), p. 122.
2. William James, "The Moral Philosopher and the Moral Life," *Essays on Faith and Morals,* edited by Ralph Barton Perry. (New York: World Publishing, 1942), p. 211.
3. Perry, vol. 2, p. 251. Emphasis in original text.

4. This is the situation, in part, that Robert Heilbroner depicts as presently confronting the human race. *An Inquiry into the Human Prospect* (New York: W. W. Norton, 1974).

5. James, *Essays,* p. 82. Emphasis in original text.

6. Ibid., p. 83.

7. Ibid.

8. James, "The Moral Philosopher and the Moral Life," *Essays,* p. 212.

9. Ibid., p. 213.

10. James, *Varieties,* p. 53.

11. Ibid., p. 56. Emphasis in original text.

12. James, *Pragmatism,* p. 188.

13. James, *Letters*, vol. 1, p. 199. Emphasis in original text.

14. James, *Varieties,* pp. 135–36.

15. Ibid., p. 136.

16. Ibid., p. 53.

17. James, *Pragmatism,* p. 78.

CHAPTER 3

1. While positivism was widespread in philosophical circles in James' day, it was with Chauncey Wright in particular that he fought his early battles on this point. For an interesting account of the relationship between these personal friends but philosophical adversaries, see Perry, vol. 1, pp. 520–32.

2. James, *Pragmatism*, p. 23.

3. James, *Letters,* vol. 1, pp. 152–53.

4. James, "Is Life Worth Living," *Essays,* pp. 24–25.

5. James, "Reflex Action and Theism," *Essays,* p. 129.

6. James, "The Dilemma of Determinism," *Essays,* p. 147.

7. While this may be a valid point, there is much more to be said in relation to it: e.g., while one might argue that our religious demands have as much right to assert themselves as our scientific ones, to what extent can we accept a religious conception of the world in the absence of the kind of verification procedures available in the natural sciences? We will return to this point later in discussing James' acceptance of God based on the need for his existence.

8. James, "Is Life Worth Living," *Essays,* p. 25.
9. James, "The Dilemma of Determinism," *Essays,* p. 147.
10. James, "Reflex Action and Theism," *Essays,* p. 132.
11. William James, *Collected Essays and Reviews,* edited by Ralph Barton Perry (New York: Russell and Russell, 1969), p. ix.
12. William James, *The Principles of Psychology* (Great Books of the Western World, edited by Robert Maynard Hutchins, Chicago: William Benton, 1952), p. 91. Emphasis in original text.
13. Ibid., p. 260. Emphasis in original text.
14. Ibid., p. 669.
15. Ibid., p 670. Emphasis in original text.
16. James, *Pragmatism,* p. 161.
17. James, *Principles,* p. 670.
18. James, "Reflex Action and Theism," *Essays,* p. 130.
19. James, *Letters,* vol. 2, p. 213.
20. As quoted in Perry, *Thought and Character,* vol. 1, p. 737.
21. James, *Letters,* vol. 2, p. 214.
22. James, *Pragmatism,* p. 77.
23. James, "The Dilemma of Determinism," *Essays,* p. 147.
24. James, "The Sentiment of Rationality," *Essays,* pp. 105–6.
25. Ibid., pp. 92–93.
26. James, "Is Life Worth Living," *Essays,* p. 31.
27. James, "Reflex Action and Theism," *Essays,* p. 141.
28. James, *Pragmatism,* p. 19.
29. Ibid.
30. James, *Letters,* vol. 2, p. 211.
31. James, *Varieties,* p. 293.
32. Ibid., pp. 323–28.
33. Ibid., p. 324.
34. Ibid., p. 327.
35. Ibid., p. 29.
36. Ibid., p. 30.
37. Ibid., p. 32.
38. Ibid., p. 391.
39. Ibid., pp. 212–13.

40. James, "The Will to Believe," *Essays,* p. 42. Emphasis in original text.
41. Ibid., p. 40.
42. Ibid., p. 59.
43. See, for example, John Hick, *Faith and Knowledge,* 2nd ed. (Ithaca: Cornell University Press, 1966), pp. 120–48.
44. James, "The Will to Believe," *Essays,* p. 32.
45. Ibid., p. 60.
46. Ibid., p. 40.
47. James, "Reflex Action and Theism," *Essays,* p. 141.
48. James, "Is Life Worth Living," *Essays,* p. 31.
49. James, *Letters,* vol. 1, pp. 152–53.
50. Ibid., p. 147.
51. James, *Essays,* p. 146.
52. Ibid.
53. James, *Varieties,* p. 330.
54. Ibid., p. 331.

CHAPTER 4

1. James, *Pragmatism,* p. 172.
2. My account here follows that of Terence Penelhum, *Religion and Rationality,* chap. 21.
3. James, "The Dilemma of Determinism," *Essays,* p. 181.
4. Jonathan Edwards, *Freedom of the Will,* edited by Paul Ramsey (New Haven: Yale University Press, 1957), pp. 239–56; 257–69.
5. James, *Pragmatism,* p. 187.
6. Ibid., pp. 190–91.
7. William James, *A Pluralistic Universe* (Gloucester, Mass.: Peter Smith, 1967), p. 30.
8. Ibid., pp. 47–48.
9. Ibid., p. 49.
10. Edward C. Moore in his work, *William James* (Great American Thinkers Series; New York: Washington Square Press, 1965), makes this point in the strongest terms. "James was unable to accept the doctrine of the impotence of man. From his rejection of this doctrine and his assertion of efficacious

powers within man himself follows almost every major tenet of his philosophy that is unique to him. It would perhaps not be an overstatement to say that James cannot argue the efficacy of human endeavor philosophically simply because it is the fundamental tenet of his position." p. 22.

11. James, *A Pluralistic Universe*, p. 117.
12. Ibid., p. 118.
13. Ibid., p. 120.
14. Ibid., p. 123.
15. James, *Varieties*, p. 115.
16. James, *A Pluralistic Universe*, p. 124.
17. Ibid., p. 25.
18. Thomas Aquinas, a most able exponent of the traditional Christian God, speaks of this God as being "in all things, and innermostly" in a causal sense. *Summa Theologica* (vol. 1, q. 8, a. 1), as found in *Basic Writings of Saint Thomas Aquinas*, ed. Anton C. Pegis (2 vols., New York: Random House, 1945), vol. 1, p. 64. He also devotes discussions to the love, justice, mercy and providence of God. *Summa Theologica* (vol. 1, qs. 20, 21, 22), *Basic Writings*, vol. 1, pp. 215–38.
19. James, *A Pluralistic Universe*, pp. 26–27.
20. James, *Pragmatism*, p. 192.
21. James, *A Pluralistic Universe*, p. 318.
22. Ibid., p. 30.
23. Ibid.
24. Ibid., chs. 4, 5.
25. Ibid., p. 168.
26. Ibid., pp. 168–69.
27. Ibid., p. 181.
28. Ibid., p. 212.
29. Ibid., p. 292.
30. Ibid., p. 310.
31. James, *Varieties*, p. 396.
32. Ibid., p. 388.
33. Ibid., pp. 392–94.
34. Ibid., p. 331.

35. James, *Pragmatism,* p. 30.
36. James, *Varieties,* p. 330.
37. Ibid., p. 346.
38. Ibid., p. 257.
39. William L. Rowe, *Religious Symbols and God* (Chicago: University of Chicago Press, 1968), p. 4.
40. Baum, pp. 162–285.
41. Macquarrie, *Thinking About God.* p. 90.

CHAPTER 5

1. William James, "Philosophical Conceptions and Practical Results," as found in *The Writings of William James,* edited by John McDermott (New York: Modern Library, 1968), p. 348.
2. Ibid., p. 349.
3. James, *Pragmatism,* p. 71.
4. Ibid., p. 77.
5. James, *Varieties,* p. 331.
6. Ibid., p. 339.
7. Ibid., p. 340.
8. James, *Pragmatism,* p. 135.
9. Ibid., p. 142.
10. Ibid., p. 167.
11. Ibid., p. 193.
12. Ibid., pp. 61–62.

CHAPTER 6

1. Paul Tillich, *The Courage to Be* (New Haven: Yale University Press, 1952), chap. 2, pp. 32–63.
2. Gilkey, p. 306.
3. See chap. 1, note 1.
4. Karl Jaspers, *Way to Wisdom* (New Haven: Yale University Press, 1954), p. 20.
5. William Barrett, *Irrational Man* (New York: Doubleday, 1958), chap. 2.
6. Michael Novak, *The Experience of Nothingness* (New York: Harper and Row, 1970.

7. Brand Blanshard, "The Opportunity of Philosophy," as found in *The Art of Philosophy,* edited by Fred A. Westphal (Englewood Cliffs, N.J.: Prentice Hall, 1972), p. 8.

8. Walter Stace, *Religion and the Modern Mind* (Philadelphia: J. B. Lippincott, 1960), pp. 56–112.

9. See, for example, William Luijpen, *Existential Phenomenology* (Pittsburgh: Duquesne University Press, 1960), pp. 25–33.

10. Perry, *Thought and Character,* vol. 2, p. 358.

11. Walter Stakes, S. J., "God for Today and Tomorrow," *The New Scholasticism,* 43 (Summer, 1969), p. 354.

12. Robert Johann, *The Pragmatic Meaning of God* (Milwaukee: Marquette University Press, 1966), p. 6.

13. Ibid., chap. 4, "Some Critical Considerations."

14. Roger A. Johnson et al., *Critical Issues in Modern Religion* (Englewood Cliffs, N.J.: Prentice Hall, 1973), pp. 443–44.

15. Stokes, "God for Today and Tomorrow," p. 362.

Bibliography

WORKS OF WILLIAM JAMES REFERRED TO IN TEXT

James, William. *Collected Essays and Reviews*. Edited by Ralph Barton Perry. New York: Longmans, Green, 1920. Reprint. New York: Russell and Russell, 1969.

_____. *Essays in Radical Empiricism*. New York: Longmans, Green, 1912.

_____. *Essays on Faith and Morals*. Edited by Ralph Barton Perry. Cleveland: World Publishing, 1942.

_____. *The Letters of William James*. 2 vols. Edited by Henry James. Boston: Atlantic Monthly Press, 1920.

_____. *A Pluralistic Universe*. New York: Longmans, Green, 1909. Reprint. Gloucester, Mass.: Peter Smith, 1967.

_____. *Pragmatism*. New York: Longmans, Green, 1907. Reprint. New York: Meridian Books, 1955.

_____. *The Principles of Psychology*. 2 vols. New York: Henry Holt and Company, 1890. Reprint. Chicago: William Benton, 1962.

_____. *The Varieties of Religious Experience*. New York: Longmans, Green, 1902. Reprint. New York: New American Library, 1958.

_____. *The Will to Believe, and Other Essays in Popular Philosophy*. New York: Longmans, Green, 1897.

_____. *The Writings of William James*. Edited by John McDermott. New York: The Modern Library, 1968.

OTHER WORKS REFERRED TO IN TEXT

Aquinas, Thomas. *Basic Writings of Saint Thomas Aquinas*. Edited by Anton Pegis. 2 vols. New York: Random House, 1945.

Barrett, William. *Irrational Man*. New York: Doubleday, 1958.

Baum, Gregory. *Man Becoming*. New York: Seabury Press, 1970.

Bixler, Julius Seelye. *Religion in the Philosophy of William James*. Boston: Marshall Jones, 1926.

Edwards, Jonathan. *Freedom of the Will*. Edited by Paul Ramsey. New Haven: Yale University Press, 1957.

Fontinell, Eugene. *Toward a Reconstruction of Religion*. New York: Doubleday, 1970.

Gilkey, Langdon. *Naming the Whirlwind: The Renewal of God Language*. Indianapolis: Bobbs Merrill, 1969.

Gill, Jerry (ed.). *Philosophy Today, No. 2*. London: Macmillan, 1969.

Heilbroner, Robert. *An Inquiry into the Human Prospect*. New York: W. W. Norton, 1974.

Hick, John. *Faith and Knowledge*. Ithaca, N.Y.: Cornell University Press, 1966.

Jaspers, Karl. *The Way to Wisdom*. New Haven: Yale University Press, 1954.

Johann, Robert. *The Pragmatic Meaning of God*. Milwaukee: Marquette University Press, 1966.

Johnson et al., Roger. *Critical Issues in Modern Religion*. Englewood Cliffs, N.J.: Prentice Hall, 1973.

Linschoten, Hans. *On the Way Toward a Phenomenological Psychology*. Pittsburgh: Duquesne University Press, 1968.

Luijpen, William. *Existential Phenomenology*. Pittsburgh: Duquesne University Press, 1960.

Macquarrie, John. *God and Secularity, New Directions in Theology Today*. Philadelphia: Westminster Press, 1967.

_____. *Thinking About God*. New York: Harper and Row, 1975.

Moore, Edward. *William James*. New York: Washington Square Press, 1965.

Novak, Michael. *The Experience of Nothingness*. New York: Harper and Row, 1970.

Penelhum, Terrence. *Religion and Rationality*. New York: Random House, 1971.

Perry, Ralph Barton. *The Thought and Character of William James*. 2 vols. Boston: Little, Brown, 1935.

Pike, Nelson. *God and Timelessness*. London: Routledge and Kegan Paul, 1970.

Rowe, William. *Religious Symbols and God*. Chicago: University of Chicago Press, 1968.

Stace, Walter. *Religion and the Modern Mind*. Philadelphia: J. B. Lippincott, 1960.

Stokes, Walter, S. J. "God for Today, and Tomorrow," *The New Scholasticism* 43 (Summer, 1969), 351–78.

Tillich, Paul. *The Courage to Be*. New Haven: Yale University Press, 1952.

————. *Systematic Theology*. 3 vols. Chicago: University of Chicago Press, 1967.

Westphal, Fred (ed.). *The Art of Philosophy*. Englewood Cliffs, N.J.: Prentice Hall, 1972.

Wild, John. *The Radical Empiricism of William James*. New York: Doubleday, 1969.

Wilshire, Bruce. *William James and Phenomenology*. Bloomington: Indiana University Press. 1968.

Index

		DATE DUE		
JUN 0 1 1992				
DEC 1 3 199?				